The Dialogue Society is a registered charity, established in London in 1999, with the aim of advancing social cohesion by connecting communities, empowering people to engage and contributing to the development of ideas on dialogue. It operates nation-wide with regional branches across the UK. Through discussion forums, courses, capacity building publications and outreach it enables people to venture across boundaries of religion, culture and social class. It provides a platform where people can meet to share narratives and perspectives, discover the values they have in common and be at ease with their differences.

www.DialogueSociety.org
info@dialoguesociety.org
Tel: +44 (0)20 7619 0361

Dialogue Society
402 Holloway Road
London N7 6PZ

Dialogue Theories

First published in Great Britain 2013

© Dialogue Society 2013

DIALOGUE
SOCIETY
LONDON 1999

Registered Charity No: 1117039

ISBN 978-0-9569304-7-7

About the authors and editor

Authors:

Frances Sleap studied Philosophy and Theology at the University of Oxford, graduating with first class honours. A master's degree in the Study of Religions gave her the opportunity to explore religions other than Christianity, feeding her interest in interfaith and intercultural relations. Since joining the Dialogue Society in spring 2010 she has worked on a range of publications, including the Community Dialogue Manuals and a booklet on 'Making Dialogue Effective'. Frances's current work includes coordinating the Dialogue Society Success School for young people and contributing to the Dialogue School for students following the MA in Dialogue Studies.

Omer Sener is a researcher and freelance writer who holds a BA in American Literature and a PhD in Cultural Studies and Literary Criticism. His research interests include ethnicity, Asian American literature, and cultural narratives. He is particularly interested in intercultural dialogue and dialogue as an academic concept across disciplines. As a Research Fellow at the Dialogue Society, he has so far worked on a number of academic publications, such as *Debating Multiculturalism I*, and written articles on the theory and practice of dialogue on the Dialogue Society website.

Editor:

Paul Weller is Professor of Inter-Religious Relations at the University of Derby, where he is Head of Research and Commercial Development in the Faculty of Education, Health and Sciences. He is a Visiting Fellow in the Oxford Centre for Christianity and Culture at Regent's Park College, University of Oxford and a founder and Trustee of the Multi-Faith Centre at the University of Derby (http://www.multifaithcentre.org). He is a member of the Advisory Board of the Dialogue Society and a Trustee of the Interreligiöse Arbeitsstelle in Germany (http://www.interrel.de). He was a founder member of the Joppa Group of Baptist Christians engaged in inter-faith dialogue and is currently a member of the Baptist Union of Great Britain's Inter-Faith Working Group. On a European level he has been a consultant to Belieforama (http://www.belieforama.eu), a community of practice based around the development of a prize-winning training programme in religious diversity and anti-discrimination.

Contents

Authors' Acknowledgements

We would like to express our heartfelt thanks to our editor Professor Paul Weller for his invaluable advice, support and belief in the project. We appreciatively acknowledge Ahmet Kurucan's assistance in providing us with his personal lecture notes on Fethullah Gülen's talks on dialogue, Ozcan Keles's valuable input on the chapter on Gülen, and Taptuk Emre Erkoc's suggestions on the chapter on Jürgen Habermas. We would also like to thank Ozcan Keles, Ilknur Kahraman and all the Dialogue Society team for their support and feedback, and for entrusting us with a fascinating and inspiring task.

Foreword

This book is part of the Dialogue Society's ongoing project of researching, promoting and contributing to dialogue. Together with the *Journal of Dialogue Studies* which will be launched this year, and the Master's in Dialogue Studies which the Dialogue Society co-delivers with Keele University, it is also intended to contribute to the development of 'Dialogue Studies' as a distinct academic field. Our hope is that focusing more attention on the academic study of dialogue will build momentum for practice as well as the development and discussion of theory. The study of dialogue would seem to have a natural place in a society oriented towards peace and inter-group respect. Perhaps it may also contribute to nurturing that orientation and creating that society.

At the Dialogue Society we are focused on addressing a deficit of dialogue before it leads to the development of conflict. Once a conflict situation arises, different mechanisms and approaches need to be employed. The question of how best to manage and resolve conflict is of course one of vital importance. However, the question of how to avoid relations breaking down to that extent in the first place deserves equal attention. Exploring dialogue theories and practices contributes to the development of better answers to that question.

In the course of our work and through interactions with other people working in the area of dialogue and good relations, we at the Dialogue Society came into contact with the work of some of the thinkers included in this volume. As we looked further, it became clear that a great number of fascinating individuals in diverse fields had thought and were thinking about dialogue. This book is intended to introduce readers to a selection of those individuals and to the rich range of theories of and insights into dialogue on offer.

A range of definitions of 'dialogue' are encompassed in this book. The Dialogue Society has its own, broad working definition. We understand dialogue to consist of meaningful interaction and exchange between people (often of different social, cultural, political, religious or professional groups) who come together through various kinds of conversations or activities with a view to increased understanding. Our approach is shaped by the thought of Islamic scholar and peace advocate Fethullah Gülen, whose work is considered in one of the chapters in this book. It is very much in keeping with his ethos for people inspired by him to reach out for further inspiration and wisdom from diverse sources.

While this book is intended to be a contribution to an emerging academic field, the authors have endeavoured to make it readable and accessible to a wide audience. In the spirit of dialogue, they and their colleagues at the Dialogue Society invite your feedback and other thoughts, which you can share by sending us an email to dialoguetheories@dialoguesociety.org.

Ozcan Keles
Executive Director

Dialogue Society
London, April 2013

Preface

It has been a privilege and pleasure to work with colleagues and friends from the Dialogue Society in the development and publication of this volume. As an Adviser to the Society I am always impressed by the energy that is evidenced in the scope of its commitment to facilitating dialogue with a wide range of individuals and groups.

But I am particularly pleased to be associated with this volume as editor. This is because, together with the new *Journal of Dialogue Studies* (of which I am Academic Editor) the Dialogue Society is seeking, through this publication, to make a contribution not only to the practice of dialogue, but also to the study of it. In doing so, it is the aim of this book both to fill a lacuna in the literature on dialogue in a way that can contribute to the academic study of it, while also being accessible to a wider public that is concerned about and (in different ways) engaged in dialogue.

The dialogue that is explored in these pages is articulated by a range of key figures from different religious, philosophical and practitioner stances. It also relates to a variety of fields of human activity. In fact, much of the thinking, questions and practical outworking of dialogue found in this volume resonate with my own personal, professional and religious history and approach. This includes the so-called 'Four Principles of Dialogue' that were developed by the former British Council of Churches' Committee for Relations with People of Other Faiths, of which I was a member in the 1980s. These principles were first articulated in a little booklet originally published in 1981 and then in a slightly revised 1983 edition, called *Relations with People of Other Faiths: Guidelines for Dialogue in Britain*. They are:

1. Dialogue begins when people meet each other.

2. Dialogue depends upon mutual understanding and mutual trust.

3. Dialogue makes it possible to share in service to the community.

4. And finally, dialogue becomes the medium of authentic witness.

These principles were initially articulated by British Christians after they set out to reflect on the (1979) *Guidelines on Dialogue* that had originally been developed by the Subunit on Dialogue with People of Living Faiths and Ideologies of the World Council of Churches. However, although their development was very much informed by Christian theological thinking, there is nothing exclusively Christian, or indeed exclusively religious, about the principles. It is in this spirit, too, that the thinkers and practitioners of dialogue whose approaches are outlined in this volume were identified – namely as those who have spoken and acted out of (different) positions of clear commitment, but whose way of speaking and acting in itself constitutes an invitation to others to join in dialogue, which is itself the ultimate aim of this book.

Professor Paul Weller
Derby, April 2013

Introduction

This book offers a short introduction to ten thinkers who have made important and insightful contributions to thinking on dialogue. It is intended to inform and inspire anyone with an interest in the meaning, value and potential of dialogue, particularly those engaged in the practice of dialogue in a professional, voluntary or personal capacity. We hope that in these pages readers will discover inspiring new thinkers to engage with, and perhaps new facets to more familiar thinkers. The book also includes discussion of a wide range of practical dialogue organisations and projects which may provide further food for thought and ideas for practice.

While it is hoped that it will be of interest to students and academics working in relevant areas, the book is not written specifically for an academic audience. No background knowledge of the area is assumed.

Each chapter is dedicated to a particular thinker and each comprises the following sections: 'Biographical Introduction', 'Thought on Dialogue', 'Theory and Practice', 'Questions for Reflection', 'Bibliography' and 'Recommended Reading'. The 'Biographical Introduction' places the thinker's ideas in the context of his/her intellectual and personal background. 'Thought on Dialogue' introduces his/her main ideas about dialogue. The 'Questions for Reflection' section offer some starting points for further reflection on the ideas introduced in the chapter. The questions are intended to provide prompts for personal or group consideration of the meaning, relevance and applications of the theories considered. While in this introductory and practically-oriented work we have not attempted to critique the thinkers considered, some of the questions provided hint at possible lines of criticism or starting points for evaluation. The bibliography simply gives full details of every source drawn upon in the chapter. 'Recommended Reading' lists the books and other resources which we would recommend as the next ports of call for interested readers. We have divided each 'Recommended Reading' section into works by the thinker in question, useful secondary sources providing commentary on his/her work, and sources giving information on practical applications of the theory. The balance of these subsections varies from chapter to chapter, depending on the availability of helpful commentary on the thinker's work, and the extent to which his/her thought has been applied in practice.

The 'Theory and Practice' sections require a little further explanation. These sections are intended to bring out the relevance of each thinker for the practice of dialogue. However, because of the diversity of the thinkers included in the book, the subject matter of this section varies somewhat from chapter to chapter. Where they or others have put their thinking into practice we report on that. In some cases we highlight practices not directly inspired by the thinker in question but reflecting similar principles or concerns. Elsewhere we have considered it helpful to give our own reflections on the relevance of the theory to dialogue practice, and on how dialogue practitioners might use the thinker's insights.

In selecting thinkers to include in the book we aimed at achieving a reasonable balance in terms of religion, culture, gender and intellectual and professional background. However in such a small selection compromises have inevitably had to be made. A second volume, should it be possible to produce one, would seek to rectify some of the obvious omissions. We decided to focus on contemporary or fairly recent thinkers,[1] since this restriction still left us with an ample choice of fascinating candidates. This said, it is worth noting that a number of the thinkers included here draw significantly on philosophers and religious teachers from more distant eras.

Our ten chosen thinkers represent diverse fields, from religious studies and interfaith dialogue, through philosophy and social theory, to communication studies, public opinion analysis and even quantum physics. As one of the ten, Daniel Yankelovich, has noted, it is striking that serious thought on dialogue has emerged out of such diverse fields, with insightful people operating in completely different contexts recognising 'something special about dialogue'.[2] Perhaps this phenomenon indicates that dialogue answers a pervasive need in contemporary society. Yankelovich sees the proliferation of dialogue initiatives in the United States as reflecting the 'existential condition' of modern America, which yearns for connection and mutual understanding in the face of the isolation accompanying trends of technological advancement, globalisation and individualism.[3] But, arguably, the 'existential condition' of contemporary American society only accentuates a perennial feature of the human existential condition. Another of our dialogue thinkers, the philosopher Martin Buber, saw dialogue as the mode of interaction which made *any* human life, in any society, worth living.

By this point, the reader may well be wondering what exactly Buber or Yankelovich mean by 'dialogue', and whether they and other thinkers are actually talking about the same thing. Is the 'dialogue' which Yankelovich sees as responding to the malaise of modern America the same 'dialogue' which Buber considers an essential element

1   Those who are not contemporary were active at least into the second half of the 20th century.

2   Daniel Yankelovich, *The Magic of Dialogue,* (New York: Simon and Schuster, 1999), 24.

3   Yankelovich, *The Magic of Dialogue,* 29 ff.

of being human? While there is important overlap between them, the thinkers examined here are not all operating with the same concept of dialogue. It does seem fair to say that all appear to see dialogue as some kind of inter-human process associated with the attainment of understanding and the fostering of empathetic relationship. However, different thinkers stress these two key elements to different degrees. For David Bohm, dialogue is essentially a process of shared thinking, in the course of which a valuable form of relationship might emerge, whereas for Buber dialogue is essentially relationship, though it generally encompasses a cognitive grasp of the other's point of view.

There is no consensus on exactly what sort of activity dialogue is. A number of our thinkers, namely, Yankelovich, O'Neill, Bohm, Armstrong and Nasr, seem to define dialogue in terms of a particular kind of conversation.[4] The conceptions of Gülen and the Dalai Lama seem to encompass a broader range of activities in which people of different cultures, religions and social, political or professional groups come together and interact. This is the sort of concept used by the Dialogue Society, which envisages dialogue as 'meaningful interaction and exchange between people (often of different social, cultural, political, religious or professional groups) who come together through various kinds of conversations or activities with a view to increased understanding.'[5] For Buber, dialogue is a mode of relating which can occur in the midst of activity or inactivity, conversation or silence.

Donal Carbaugh's perspective on dialogue is unique in this volume. While others set out their own ideal of dialogue, his work examines and describes the concept of 'dialogue' or equivalent notions that exist in different cultures. His findings highlight the fact that we have just noted in relation to the thinkers considered in this book: we cannot assume that everyone means the same thing by 'dialogue'. This is an important point for practitioners to bear in mind; the particular form of dialogue that we see as an optimal form of communication may be alien and unappealing to the people of a different group with whom we wish to engage. In imposing a particular model without ascertaining its acceptability for all those concerned we may find ourselves embarking on intercultural dialogue in a culturally insensitive manner.

The diverse thinkers we have included could have been grouped in a number of different ways. We have chosen simply to order them alphabetically and allow

---

4   Our chapter on Habermas also deals with kinds of conversation. However, we should note that Habermas himself writes not of 'dialogue' but of 'argumentation' and speech in the context of 'communicative action'.

5   'About Us,' Dialogue Society, accessed 25th March 2013, http://www.dialoguesociety.org/about-us.html.

readers to explore and enjoy the diverse connections between them. We begin with Karen Armstrong, a writer on religion and former Roman Catholic nun, whose understanding of dialogue is deeply connected with her vision of the compassionate life. Her work draws on the wisdom of a diverse range of great thinkers and religious teachers. Our second thinker, the innovative physicist David Bohm, offers a model of dialogue as 'thinking together' which he himself explored in practice. He believed that dialogue could help us to understand the often incoherent ways in which we think, helping us to address the root causes of a range of contemporary problems. Next, we explore Martin Buber's powerful vision of dialogue as a fundamental form of relating to the other, the mode of being that makes us human. Then we take a look at dialogue from a communication studies perspective, exploring Donal Carbaugh's insights on the meaning of 'dialogue' in different cultural systems. Our fifth thinker is Fethullah Gülen, the Turkish Islamic scholar and peace advocate who has inspired an international movement of dialogue and education initiatives. We explore his philosophy of dialogue, grounded in a profound sense of the primacy of our common humanity and in a cluster of virtues characterising 'people of the heart'.

Next we come to Tenzin Gyatso, the Fourteenth Dalai Lama, identifying the principles expounded in his speeches and writings and exemplified in his practice of dialogue. We analyse his direct, compassionate style of engagement in interfaith contexts, in situations of conflict and in encounters between science and religion. We then move on to the eminent social theorist Jürgen Habermas, examining his model of rational, transparent and courteous communication. Subsequently we consider the Muslim intellectual Seyyed Hossein Nasr's view of dialogue in the interfaith context, coloured by his keen sense of common spiritual ground between different religious traditions. We also take a look at his view of the kind of dialogical relationship that needs to exist between science and religion. Our penultimate chapter explores Maura O'Neill's insights on dialogue, based on her extensive experience of women's participation in interfaith dialogue. She alerts us to key considerations concerning the barriers that may inhibit free participation in dialogue, and the potential benefits of efforts to ensure true inclusivity. Finally, we consider leading public opinion analyst Daniel Yankelovich's definition of dialogue, his suggestion of strategies through which it can be achieved, and his vision of the role it may play in revitalising democracy.

As already mentioned, it is hoped that these theories of dialogue will provide dialogue practitioners with inspiration and new ideas, and the 'Theory and Practice' sections specifically seek to relate the thinkers' ideas to practice. The thinkers included have diverse relationships with dialogue practice. Some of them, like Habermas and Buber, present shining visions of dialogue as a uniquely valuable form of human interaction, portraying the image of the ideal more fully than the mechanics of attaining it. Others carefully bring to our attention some of the concrete difficulties that may be encountered in dialogue; O'Neill explores the profound impact of gender inequality, Yankelovich provides a catalogue of dialogue 'pitfalls' and Carbaugh explores the scope for intercultural confusion.

Some critics of dialogue theorists, such as Michel Foucault, whose challenge to Habermas is touched upon in this volume, see certain theories of dialogue as naive and unattainable illusions that overlook the pervasive human realities of power imbalances and manipulation. Certainly, these phenomena pose real challenges both to the theorists and to practitioners. However, the practitioners we mention in our 'Theory and Practice' sections testify to the usefulness of striving for an ideal, even when it is very hard fully to attain. It is certainly very important to keep in mind the myriad complications and challenges involved in dialogue, as highlighted by some of our thinkers, and by critics. Nevertheless, in our view, they are not grounds for relinquishing the challenges involved in dialogue.

Readers will discover in these pages a range of notable parallels between the thought of these thinkers drawn from such diverse fields and cultures. Former nun Karen Armstrong and the Dalai Lama share the same deep sense of the connection between dialogue and an underlying outlook of compassion, which can be cultivated through practice and commitment. Exploring reports of encounters with the Dalai Lama, one cannot but see him as an expert in the dialogic connection described by Buber. Gülen and Buber share a commitment to the development of education, and a profound sense of the educator's role in introducing children to dialogical attitudes.

It is also notable that these thinkers are in the habit of explicitly drawing on each other and on other dialogue thinkers. Karen Armstrong casts her net wide across the sea of religious teachers and philosophers; Yankelovich draws on Buber and Habermas; Bohm engaged in fruitful dialogue with both the Dalai Lama and with the Indian spiritual teacher Jiddu Krishnamurti. Of course, from such deeply dialogical individuals we would expect nothing less.

Karen Armstrong

Biographical Introduction

Karen Armstrong is a renowned British writer on religion whose writings have earned her respect among people of different faith traditions. She has written books on world religions, on their histories and on prominent figures within them.

A former Roman Catholic nun, Armstrong's varied personal experiences with religion have had an important impact on her writing, which promotes interfaith understanding and dialogue. When she was seventeen years old she entered the Roman Catholic order of the Society of the Holy Child Jesus, taking vows of poverty and chastity.[1] She left the order after seven years, in 1969. She gained a congratulatory first class honours degree in English Literature from Oxford University and later went on to become a broadcaster and a full-time author.[2] In her first book, *Through the Narrow Gate*, published in 1982, she wrote about her life in the convent.[3] Two years later she was commissioned to make a documentary chronicling the life of St Paul. Her research for this project in the Middle East inspired her to undertake further research on the Abrahamic religions. She has written sixteen books to date[4] including the best-selling *A History of God* which was the basis of a 2001 History Channel feature-length documentary film. Her scholarship on the three Abrahamic religions of Islam, Judaism, and Christianity has resulted in her acknowledgement as 'a major contributor to interfaith understanding and respect.'[5]

Although Armstrong does not always directly use the word 'dialogue' in her writings, her long study of diverse faiths gives her a valuable perspective on dialogue and understanding between people of different convictions. In her book *Twelve Steps to a Compassionate Life*, she focuses on the concept of compassion articulated in different faith traditions and explores how one can cultivate compassionate attitudes and practices. Dialogue, a compassionate way of speaking with one another, is introduced as an essential element of a compassionate life. Armstrong discusses the

---

1   'Karen Armstrong, Biography and Resources,' Enlightennext.org, accessed 4th July, 2012, http://www.enlightennext.org/magazine/bios/karen-armstrong.asp.

2   Armstrong, *Twelve Steps to a Compassionate Life* (Bodley Head, 2011), endpaper.

3   'Karen Armstrong: Religious Scholar,' TED, accessed 6th July, 2012, http://www.ted.com/speakers/karen_armstrong.html.

4   Karen Armstrong, *Twelve Steps to a Compassionate Life*, endpaper.

5   'Karen Armstrong, Biography and Resources,' Enlightennext.org, accessed 4th July, 2012, http://www.enlightennext.org/magazine/bios/karen-armstrong.asp.

philosophy of dialogue as practised by Socrates, the Buddha and Confucius. The book explicitly targets people of all faiths and none. Armstrong's writings and this work in particular are written in an accessible style and have an inspirational appeal for a wide readership.

Twelve Steps to a Compassionate Life was written as part of an extensive project to propagate compassion. The project was undertaken with the support of an award from TED (Technology, Entertainment, Design), a non-profit organisation 'devoted to ideas worth spreading', which gives an annual award to an individual with an idea capable of making a difference in the world.[6]

---

6   TED began its existence as a conference in 1984 aiming to bring together people from technology, entertainment and design backgrounds, hence its title. Since then, TED has developed to become an international phenomenon open to good ideas from a much broader range of fields. It now runs two annual conferences, an annual TED prize, and a TED Talks video website accessible across the globe. 'About TED,' TED, accessed 15th Oct, 2012, http://www.ted.com/pages/about; 'Karen Armstrong wins the TED Prize,' Charter for Compassion, accessed 20th March, 2013, http://charterforcompassion.org/the-charter/historic-moments/2.

Thought on Dialogue

Our main source in exploring Armstrong's thoughts on dialogue is her book *Twelve Steps to a Compassionate Life*. It was written as part of Armstrong's Charter for Compassion project, supported by TED. Its overall aim is to encourage commitment to and cultivation of the essential virtue of compassion, a virtue which is indispensable to the practice of dialogue as understood by Armstrong.

For Armstrong, compassion is 'an attitude of principled, consistent altruism' based on empathic consideration of others people's points of view.[7] From the outset Armstrong stresses that the principle of compassion is present as a key value at the core of each religious tradition. In each we find some version of 'the Golden Rule', the principle, 'Do to others as you would want them to do to you,' also known by its negative counterpart, 'Do not do to others what you would not wish them to do to you.' Throughout the book Armstrong draws on a range of thinkers, philosophers and major religious figures, from Socrates, the Buddha and Confucius to Jesus Christ and Prophet Muhammed. She also draws powerfully on personal experience.

As well as offering helpful insights on compassion drawn from diverse sources, Armstrong suggests reflective exercises through which individuals may develop compassionate attitudes and habits. She argues that compassion is a natural component of human beings which, like any ability, can be nurtured and developed through effort and practice.[8] The exercises suggested are intended to support that effort and practice.

One chapter of the book in particular, entitled 'How Should We Speak to One Another?' is essentially devoted to the philosophy and practice of dialogue. We will be paying particular attention to that chapter in our exploration of Armstrong's understanding of dialogue. However, if we accept Armstrong's view that dialogue involves a compassionate attitude,[9] it becomes clear that the whole book is relevant to dialogue, since it analyses this compassionate attitude and helps readers to cultivate it. We might say that the whole book elaborates an ethos for dialogue. After examining Armstrong's thoughts on 'how we should speak to one another' we will briefly consider some of the other aspects of compassion explored in the book which are of particular interest in relation to the practice of dialogue.

Turning now to Armstrong's understanding of dialogue as given in chapter 8 of

---

7   Armstrong, *Twelve Steps to a Compassionate Life*, 6.

8   Armstrong, *Twelve Steps to a Compassionate Life*, 17 f.

9   Armstrong, *Twelve Steps to a Compassionate Life*, 121 ff, especially 128-9.

Twelve Steps, we find that Armstrong bases her perspective on dialogue partly on the ideal of Socratic Dialogue. Under the heading, 'How Should We Speak to One Another?' Armstrong argues that the practice of 'Socratic dialogue' has been lost in the contemporary world. Most of modern discourse is characterised by fierce debate, rhetoric and demagogy, features reminiscent of political debates among the Ancient Greeks, which the philosopher Socrates experienced and disliked.[10] It is combative, aggressive, and all about winning the argument. While, in some contexts, such discourse serves a purpose, it does not change people's minds or address conflicts and divisions. We badly need to rediscover Socrates' alternative to this form of discourse.

'Socratic dialogue' is, in essence, a spiritual exercise that brings a profound recognition of ignorance, which in turn makes way for the quest for truth. It involves politely trying to understand the other side. It 'must be conducted with gentleness and without malice.'[11] In this type of dialogue, which Armstrong promotes, the participants do not try to win over each other in a heated argument, as in the previously mentioned political debates of the Athenians.[12] Rather, they try to communicate clearly and considerately and to understand and empathise with one another. Armstrong shows that many of the key features of Socratic dialogue are also found in the approaches and practices of other great sages, including Confucius and the Buddha. It is also worth noting here Armstrong's observation in another work that the three Abrahamic traditions of Judaism, Islam and Christianity are all based on a dialogue between God and human beings.[13]

In accordance with its different goal, Socratic dialogue is conducted in a very different spirit to the debates of ancient Athens and to much contemporary discourse. The goal is not to win the argument but to work together towards the discovery of truth. Participants engage with the views and questions surfacing in the dialogue and allow their thinking to be changed as a result of the dialogue process.[14] Socratic dialogue with others can enable participants to enter into dialogue with themselves, to question and re-evaluate long-held preconceptions and biases. In so doing they gain an appreciation of the limitations of their own knowledge. They are 'taken beyond themselves' and thus come to a realisation that they need to increase

---

10   Armstrong, *Twelve Steps to a Compassionate Life*, 121.

11   Armstrong, 'Charter for Compassion: At One with Our Ignorance,' *The Guardian*, 10th November, 2009, accessed 5th July, 2012, http://www.guardian.co.uk/commentisfree/belief/2009/nov/10/charter-for-compassion-our-ignorance.

12   Armstrong, *Twelve Steps to a Compassionate Life*, 121.

13   Armstrong, *A History of God* (Vintage, 1999), 250.

14   Armstrong, *Twelve Steps to a Compassionate Life*, 122.

in wisdom and understanding.[15] This dialogue does not necessarily require us to change all our opinions and abandon our worldview. However, it does require that we be prepared to move beyond our conventional 'habitual thinking'.[16] We have to be ready to step outside our mental comfort zones and look at our own opinions and ideas from a new perspective. One of the aims of Socratic dialogue is thus to transform the individual participant and create a more 'authentic self'.[17] This transformation stemming from dialogue can even have the positive outcome of making those involved in it happy.[18] Socratic dialogue, then, is a 'spiritual exercise', a 'communal meditation' that leads to new insights and personal growth.[19]

In Armstrong's description of this kind of dialogue a number of key characteristics are identified without which a shared spiritual quest for truth would be impossible. Let us briefly analyse these key requirements.

Firstly, this kind of dialogue must be conducted in the spirit of a conversation between friends. It takes patience, understanding and generosity. Participants must not push others to the fringes and force them to accept unwanted positions, or push their own views upon others; rather, the dialogue should be conducted in a polite, compassionate manner.[20] Participants should be able to 'maintain… a disciplined, open-hearted accord.'[21] They must shy away from any temptation to flatter their own ego by highlighting the errors of others, or to deliberately use words to harm the other person, to inflame the discussion or to incite a quarrel.[22] We see parallels to this approach in the teachings and actions of Confucius and of the Buddha. Confucius taught his pupils in a way that allowed them to develop their abilities by learning from other people's points of view, through 'friendly interaction', without harassment. The Buddha taught his disciples to be polite and understanding in their interactions.[23]

Another requirement for dialogue is that participants must listen intently to others'

---

15   Armstrong, 'Charter for Compassion: At One with Our Ignorance.'

16   Armstrong, *Twelve Steps to a Compassionate Life*, 150.

17   Armstrong, *Twelve Steps to a Compassionate Life*, 110.

18   Armstrong, *The Case for God: What Religion Really Means* (London: Knopf, 2009), 64.

19   Armstrong, *The Case for God: What Religion Really Means*, 65; *Twelve Steps to a Compassionate Life*, 122.

20   Armstrong, *Twelve Steps to a Compassionate Life*, 122; Armstrong, *The Case for God: What Religion Really Means*, 68.

21   Armstrong, *The Case for God: What Religion Really Means*, 68.

22   Armstrong, *Twelve Steps to a Compassionate Life*, 130.

23   Armstrong, *Twelve Steps to a Compassionate Life*, 122-123.

positions. We should not, as in a debate or discussion, try to manipulate the words of others in order to strengthen our argument and weaken the other's position.[24] Those involved in dialogue should be able to listen to each other say what they have to say without unnecessary interruption and without denouncing their arguments as false or not worth listening to. This principle of dialogue is as important in interactions between states as it is in intimate conversations between individuals.[25]

A further prerequisite of establishing a healthy dialogue is a certain level of mutual trust. The assumption that the other speaker is telling the truth and is worth listening to is necessary to make dialogue possible.[26] If we do not trust the person with whom we are in dialogue, and cannot find some truth and reason in her or his discourse we will eventually, in Armstrong's words, 'dismiss the speaker as irrational, nonsensical and basically inhuman,'[27] destroying any chance of establishing meaningful dialogue.

In Armstrong's vision, dialogue, or 'compassionate discourse'[28] is intimately connected to other aspects of compassionate life. Notably, it both requires and helps us to achieve a proper appreciation of how little we know, which is also one of the twelve steps.[29] This sense of the limitations of our own knowledge enables us to 'make place for the other', which is essential in dialogue. It can be cultivated by meditative practices and deliberate imaginative efforts to step outside our own point of view,[30] as well as by the process of dialogue itself, in which we open ourselves and our preconceptions to questioning. Armstrong notes that in the sphere of religion a considerable degree of ignorance is inevitable: 'We can never understand the transcendence we call God, Nirvana, Brahman or Dao, precisely because it *is* transcendent.'[31] Consciousness of this inescapable ignorance is a valuable safeguard against arrogance in interfaith dialogue.

Also particularly valuable for dialogue with people of different religions, or indeed different cultures, ethnicities or nationalities, is the cultivation of concern for everybody, another of Armstrong's steps. She writes of the necessity of reaching out to the other and of having concern for people and groups who are outside our

---

24   Armstrong, *Twelve Steps to a Compassionate Life*, 126.

25   Armstrong, *Twelve Steps to a Compassionate Life*, 172.

26   Armstrong, *Twelve Steps to a Compassionate Life*, 127.

27   Armstrong, *Twelve Steps to a Compassionate Life*, 128.

28   Armstrong, *Twelve Steps to a Compassionate Life*, 125.

29   Armstrong, *Twelve Steps to a Compassionate Life*, 106 ff.

30   Armstrong, *Twelve Steps to a Compassionate Life*, 112 f.

31   Armstrong, *Twelve Steps to a Compassionate Life*, 108.

immediate surroundings. Citing a Qur'anic verse on diversity, Armstrong argues that it is our duty to get to know one another, develop an appreciation of 'the essential unity and equality of the entire human family' and 'cultivate a concern and responsibility for *all* our neighbours' all around the world.[32] An effort to understand and reach out to the 'other' is of utmost importance, especially in the contemporary world which is more interconnected than ever.[33]

As part of a reflective exercise to cultivate concern for all, Armstrong advises readers to listen carefully to the discourse of those in our surroundings who incite hatred towards other worldviews, faiths and ethnic groups. This 'dehumanizing discourse', which is completely contrary to the spirit of dialogue, utilises words and phrases that show 'disgust and contempt' of other groups, undermining and overwhelming them. It is this kind of discourse, Armstrong notes, which made possible such atrocities as 'the enslavement and oppression of African and Native Americans... the Shoah... and the mass killings in Bosnia.'[34] In seeking compassionate dialogue across boundaries of culture, ethnicity and religion we must be alert to such discourse and abstain from it utterly. Dialogue should be infused by a concern for all which recognises and rejects tribal discourse and behaviour.

Another of the twelve steps essential to Socratic dialogue as understood by Armstrong is empathy. She understands empathy as the ability to use your imagination and put yourself in others' shoes, opening yourself to their concerns and to their sufferings.[35] Dialogue in which people seek truth together cannot proceed on the basis of mere hearsay and speculation about the other's position and world view; those engaged in dialogue must attempt really to understand the other. They must loosen their grip on their own preconceptions and outlooks sufficiently to 'make place for the other'.[36] By adopting this approach they can start to achieve an understanding of the other individual, country or tradition.[37]

Often dialogue will only get off the ground if we give serious consideration to the perspective of others involved and their psychological positions. Armstrong gives the example of the dialogue between the Buddha and the King of Kosala. The king asks the Buddha's advice about his preoccupation with himself. The Buddha, in reply, does not lecture him on lofty spiritual ideals. He empathises

---

32   Armstrong, *Twelve Steps to a Compassionate Life*, 133.

33   Armstrong, *Twelve Steps to a Compassionate Life*, 133-134.

34   Armstrong, *Twelve Steps to a Compassionate Life*, 136.

35   Armstrong, *Twelve Steps to a Compassionate Life*, 82 ff.

36   Armstrong, *Twelve Steps to a Compassionate Life*, 106.

37   Armstrong, *Twelve Steps to a Compassionate Life*, 148-9.

with the king, recognises his preoccupations and takes them as a starting point. He advises him to reflect on his own love for himself and appreciate that other individuals love themselves just as he does. Through this appreciation, based upon his own experience, he can learn not to 'harm the self of others' but to treat them with kindness and respect. The Buddha's teaching method, based upon empathic understanding, helps the king in a way that impersonal argumentation could not.[38]

Armstrong considers that even where the other's position is morally objectionable, we need to respond with empathy and find a way of posing Socratic questions and exploring his and our positions together. Armstrong illustrates this point through the example of her own dealings with analysts who cling to a stereotypical image of Islam as violent and intolerant. Her own rational counterarguments were, she considers, often counter-productive. Such dialogue, based on persuading the other side that they are wrong, only makes them more fierce and uncompromising in their verdict. Armstrong suggests that a much more fruitful approach is to empathise with the position of such opponents, 'start from where they are rather than where we think they ought to be,' and pose respectful but searching questions. This approach may 'lead to personal insight'.[39]

Armstrong's chapter on the last of her twelve steps, 'Love Your Enemies', also offers insights of real importance to dialogue, especially in the context of conflict. At the outset she underlines the urgency of the need to find alternatives to violent conflict. Citing the Dalai Lama, who considers war an 'outdated' concept, she argues that in the contemporary globalised world warfare is no longer a viable option.[40] Violence against another nation will inevitably lead to harm to our own. Restraining retaliatory instincts and extending empathy to the enemy is taxing but indispensable. In Martin Luther King's words, '"forgiving those who inflict evil and injury on us... is an absolute necessity for our survival."'[41] Dialogue is the alternative to violence that is needed, but it will only be effective if it is rooted in compassion towards the 'enemy'. She suggests reflective exercises to cultivate compassion towards enemies, based on recognition of our own hostility and efforts to imaginatively enter into the other's position. By trying to understand the suffering and pain of the other, we may access the understanding of their position which opens the way to reconciliation, real dialogue, and hope.[42]

---

38   Armstrong, *Twelve Steps to a Compassionate Life*, 123.

39   Armstrong, *Twelve Steps to a Compassionate Life*, 126.

40   Armstrong, *Twelve Steps to a Compassionate Life*, 163.

41   Armstrong, *Twelve Steps to a Compassionate Life*, 167.

42   Armstrong, *Twelve Steps to a Compassionate Life*, 171 f.

Theory and Practice

The whole of Armstrong's *Twelve Steps to a Compassionate Life,* in which she presents her vision of dialogue as compassionate discourse, has an intensely practical focus. Her reflections and the reflective practices she recommends are intended to help people undertake the 'lifelong project' of becoming compassionate human beings, capable of offering 'a haven of peace in a violent, angry world.'[43] She seeks to help people make their actions and speech a force for good, inspired by transformative encounters with compassion in her own life.

She recounts one such encounter with an elderly nun during her own time as a nun. When this woman, who had been suffering terribly from cancer for many months, was close to passing away, Armstrong and other young nuns went to her sick bed to bid her a final farewell. As they were leaving the room, the elderly nun took the trouble to call Armstrong back. She told her that although she had been warned by Armstrong's previous superiors that she may be difficult, she was never a problem for her, and had always been 'a good girl'.[44] Armstrong recounts how this act of kindness strengthened her and remained with her through life, providing encouragement whenever she felt negative and hopeless.[45] The encounter illustrates Armstrong's sense that a compassionate action can provide a unique, precious 'spot of time' in someone's life that can provide healing and strength and change that person's life for the better. We are all capable of offering such invaluable gifts to others, Armstrong holds. We will be better able to do so if through 'disciplined, repetitive action', we build positive traits and establish the habit of 'lighten[ing] [others'] lives with acts of friendship'.[46]

Each of the chapters in *Twelve Steps* closes with suggested activities or reflective exercises which can help us to establish positive habits. In the eighth step, Armstrong suggests exercises to help us focus on and improve the way in which we speak to one another.

She suggests questions for us to reflect upon, enquiring from the reader:

> [w]hen you argue, do you get carried away by your own cleverness and deliberately inflict pain on your opponent? Do you get personal? Will the points you make further the cause of understanding or are they exacerbating an already inflammatory situation? Are you really listening open-heartedly to your opponent? What would happen if... you allowed yourself to lose the argument?[47]

---

43   Armstrong, *Twelve Steps to a Compassionate Life,* 176, 178.

44   Armstrong, *Twelve Steps to a Compassionate Life,* 101.

45   Armstrong, *Twelve Steps to a Compassionate Life,* 101.

46   Armstrong, *Twelve Steps to a Compassionate Life,*102-103.

47   Armstrong, *Twelve Steps to a Compassionate Life,* 130.

She suggests that after a heated conversation we should analyse the way in which we engaged: '[C]an you really back up everything you said in the heat of the moment? Did you really know what you were talking about, or were you depending on 'hearsay'?'[48]

As a helpful checklist of principles for compassionate discourse, Armstrong cites St Paul's statement on the characteristics of love. Love, according to St Paul, involves kindness and patience and is never boastful, conceited or rude. Further, it "takes no pleasure in the wrongdoing of others"'; it is not self-righteous.[49] In dialogue we need to continuously check whether we have fallen into the trap of trying to inflate our own ego by focusing on the faults of others.

As mentioned in the introduction to this chapter, the *Twelve Steps* book is part of a broader initiative of action to propagate compassion. With the help of her award from TED, Armstrong launched the Charter for Compassion, described on its own website as follows: 'The Charter for Compassion is a document that transcends religious, ideological, and national differences. Supported by leading thinkers from many traditions, the Charter activates the Golden Rule around the world.'[50] The great contemporary need for this kind of work is summed up in the Charter itself: 'We urgently need to make compassion a clear, luminous and dynamic force in our polarized world. Rooted in a principled determination to transcend selfishness, compassion can break down political, dogmatic, ideological and religious boundaries.'[51]

The Charter was created through a highly dialogical process. Thousands of people from over one hundred countries responded to the initial appeal for contributions to the Charter via a multi-lingual website. Many thousands more commented on the original contributions. The Charter was finalised through a dialogue among the 'Council of Conscience,' a multi-faith, multi-national group of religious thinkers and leaders,' including the Grand Mufti of the Arab Republic of Egypt, Sheikh Ali Gomaa, Sister Joan Chittister, Archbishop Desmond Tutu and Rabbi Awraham Soetendorp.[52] Dialogue on compassion and how to propagate it continues online and at book groups across the world in which participants read and discuss the

---

48   Armstrong, *Twelve Steps to a Compassionate Life*, 130-131.

49   Armstrong, *Twelve Steps to a Compassionate Life*, 129.

50   'The Charter for Compassion,' Charter for Compassion, accessed 6th July, 2012, http://charterforcompassion.org/the-charter/#charter-for-compassion.

51   Armstrong, *Twelve Steps to a Compassionate Life*, 5.

52   'Council of Conscience,' Charter for Compassion, accessed 15th February, 2013, http://charterforcompassion.org/the-charter/council-of-conscience.

Twelve Steps book.[53]

The Charter is not only a written document; the initiative has brought together over 150 partners worldwide committed to 'translat[ing] the charter into practical, realistic action.'[54] Compassionate Action Network International 'facilitates' the Charter, connecting and supporting initiatives across the world in sectors from religion to business to education. Partners are engaged in a wide range of initiatives, from addressing the injustice of poverty to promoting tolerance through media. Over 80 cities have signed up to a Campaign for Compassionate Cities. In each, groups of citizens decide on and implement their own compassionate initiatives, from mass volunteering drives to creative arts projects. In Pakistan the Ali Hasan Mangi Memorial Trust is assisting Khairo Dero village in becoming an official 'compassionate village'. New education, health and other facilities are being developed in the village at the same time as social and arts initiatives on the theme of compassion.[55]

A number of the Charter's partners are specifically focused on dialogue. 20,000 Dialogues describes itself as 'a nationwide [United States] initiative that uses films to facilitate dialogue about Muslims and Islam.'[56] It provides films and other resources to volunteer hosts who lead interfaith conversations in their local areas with a view to promoting understanding, friendship and peace. At the Jewish-Palestinian Living Room Dialogue Group on the San Francisco Peninsula, American Jews and Palestinians engage in a Sustained Dialogue process, 'continually learning to change strangers into friends and "enemies" into partners, moving from confrontation to collaboration and concrete projects to help people and the public peace process, here and overseas.'[57]

---

53   'News and Events,' Charter for Compassion, accessed 15th Oct, 2012, http://charterforcompassion.org/news-and-events/index/Event.

54   Armstrong, *Twelve Steps to a Compassionate Life*, 5.

55   'Compassionate Schools: Khairo Dero Village,' Charter for Compassion, accessed 6th July, 2012, http://charterforcompassion.org/news-and-events/article/105.

56   20000 Dialogues, accessed 16th February, 2013, http://www.20000dialogues.org/.

57   'Jewish –Palestinian Living Room Dialogue Group', Charter for Compassion, accessed 16th February, 2013, http://charterforcompassion.org/our-partners/partner/65. Sustained Dialogue is a five-stage dialogue process designed by Harold H. Saunders, which aims to transform relationships and bring about change: International Institute for Sustained Dialogue, accessed 20th March, 2013, www.sustaineddialogue.org.

Bay NVC[58] offers training, facilitation, counselling, mediation and conflict resolution services using the principles and methods of Nonviolent Communication (NVC), also known as 'Compassionate Communication'. The description of the NVC approach on the website of the international Centre for Nonviolent Communication is very reminiscent of the ideal of compassionate discourse offered in Armstrong's *Twelve Steps*: 'It is based on historical principles of nonviolence- the natural state of compassion when no violence is present in the heart… With NVC we learn to hear our own deeper needs and those of others. Through its emphasis on deep listening—to ourselves as well as others—NVC helps us discover the depth of our own compassion.'[59]

Armstrong, the Council of Compassion and the partners and signatories of the Charter continue their efforts to build commitment to compassion worldwide. Dialogue, compassionate discourse, as an integral element of compassionate living, is an integral aspect of these efforts.

---

58   'Bay NVC,' Charter for Compassion, accessed 16th February, 2013, http:// charterforcompassion.org/our-partners/partner/14.

59   'What is NVC,' The Center for Nonviolent Communication, accessed 16th February 2013, http://www.cnvc.org/about/what-is-nvc.html.

Questions for Reflection

1. Socrates considered that dialogue involves the realisation that we know nothing. (Having realised my own ignorance I can begin to seek real insight and truth.)

   a. Is this profound recognition of ignorance compatible with religious conviction?

   b. In an interfaith context, in which participants are concerned to recognise and respect one another's religious convictions, to what extent can dialogue be Socratic?

2. Armstrong advocates compassionate dialogue even with uncompromising people whose ideas we find hateful. It is, she says, more helpful to engage with these people's underlying fears than to simply try to refute them.

   a. How do we balance the concern to stand up for justice and truth with the concern to maintain compassionate dialogue with everyone?

   b. Are there contexts in which compassionate dialogue is not the most helpful, or even the most compassionate response?

3. Armstrong notes that aggressive debate dominates today's politics just as it dominated the politics of Socrates' Athenian society.

   a. Can politics ever become more dialogical?

   b. What would a more dialogical politics look like?

4. How can an individual cultivate the habit of compassionate communication?

5. How might the same practice be cultivated in a whole society?

Bibliography

20000 Dialogues. Accessed 16th February, 2013. http://www.20000dialogues.org/.

Armstrong, Karen. *A History of God: The 4000-year Quest of Judaism, Christianity and Islam*. London: Vintage, 1999.

Armstrong, Karen. 'Charter for Compassion: At One with our Ignorance.' *The Guardian,* 10th November, 2009. Accessed 5th July, 2012. http://www.guardian.co.uk/commentisfree/belief/2009/nov/10/charter-for-compassion-our-ignorance.

Armstrong, Karen. *The Case for God*. London: Knopf, 2009.

Armstrong, Karen. *Twelve Steps to a Compassionate Life*. London: Bodley Head, 2011.

Center for Nonviolent Communication, The. 'What is NVC.' Accessed 16th February, 2013. http://www.cnvc.org/about/what-is-nvc.html.

Charter for Compassion. 'Bay NVC.' Accessed 16th February, 2013. http://charterforcompassion.org/our-partners/partner/14.

Charter for Compassion. 'Council of Conscience.' Accessed 15th February, 2013. http://charterforcompassion.org/the-charter/council-of-conscience.

Charter for Compassion. 'Jewish – Palestinian Living Room Dialogue Group.' Accessed 16th February, 2013. http://charterforcompassion.org/our-partners/partner/65.

Charter for Compassion. 'Karen Armstrong wins the TED Prize.' Accessed 20th March, 2013. http://charterforcompassion.org/the-charter/historic-moments/2.

Enlightennext.org. 'Karen Armstrong, Biography and Resources'. Accessed 4th July, 2012. http://www.enlightennext.org/magazine/bios/karen-armstrong.asp.

Mangi, Naween. 'Khairo Dero's Children Stage Compassionate Living Day.' Charter of Compassion. Accessed 5th July, 2012. http://charterforcompassion.org/news-and-events/article/105.

Sustained Dialogue. Accessed 16th February, 2013. http://www.sustaineddialogue.org/.

Recommended Reading

Armstrong's Works:

Armstrong, Karen. *A History of God: The 4000-year Quest of Judaism, Christianity and Islam*. London: Vintage, 1999.

Armstrong, Karen. 'Do unto Others.' *The Guardian,* 14th November, 2008. Accessed 5th July, 2012. http://www.guardian.co.uk/commentisfree/2008/nov/14/religion.

Armstrong, Karen. *Jerusalem: One City, Three Faiths.* New York: Knopf, 1996.

Armstrong, Karen. *The Spiral Staircase.* New York: Anchor Books, 2005.

Armstrong, Karen. *Through the narrow gate: a nun's story.* London: MacMillan, 1982.

Armstrong, Karen. *Twelve Steps to a Compassionate Life.* London: Bodley Head, 2011.

Armstrong, Karen. 'Why is the Charter for Compassion so Important?' *Huffington Post*, 18th November, 2008. Accessed 5th July, 2012. http://www.huffingtonpost.com/karen-armstrong/why-is-the-charter-for- co_b_144666.html.

Interfaithing. 'Karen Armstrong: Socratic Dialogue.' Accessed 5th July, 2012. http://www.interfaithing.com/karen-armstrong-socratic-dialogue-300/.

Commentary:

Brunton, Michael. 'The reason of faith.' *Odewire*, September-October 2009. Accessed 18th February, 2013. http://odewire.com/57655/the-reason-of-faith.html.

'Desert Island Discs: Karen Armstrong.' *Desert Island Discs.* BBC Radio 4. Sunday 12th February, 2006. Accessed 18th February, 2013. http://www.bbc.co.uk/radio4/features/desert-island-discs/castaway/d7f82254.

James, Patrick. 'Compassion: Karen Armstrong on Interfaith Dialogue.' Good, 18th December, 2008. Accessed 5th July, 2012. http://www.good.is/post/compassion-karen-armstrong-on-interfaith-dialogue/.

Practical Applications:

20000 Dialogues. Accessed 16th February, 2013. http://www.20000dialogues.org/.

Bay Area Nonviolent Communication. Accessed 16th February, 2013. http://baynvc.org/.

Center for Nonviolent Communication, the. Accessed 16th February, 2013. http://www.cnvc.org/about/what-is-nvc.html.

Charter for Compassion. Accessed 16th February, 2013. http://charterforcompassion.org.

Our Jewish-Palestinian Living Room Dialogue Group in California. Accessed 16th February, 2013. http://traubman.igc.org/dg-prog.htm.

David Bohm

Biographical Introduction

David Bohm (d. 1992) was a specialist in quantum physics who explored new thinking in the sciences. He was born 20th December, 1917, in Wilkes-Barre, Pennsylvania to a Hungarian father and Lithuanian mother. His early attraction to science stemmed from the science fiction books that he enjoyed reading from an early age.[1] He started his scientific career in the USA but subsequently worked in a range of countries including Brazil and the UK.

Bohm took up a post as Professor of Theoretical Physics at Birkbeck College in London in 1961 and remained in England until he passed away.[2] During these last thirty years of his life Bohm conducted research mainly on quantum theory and relativity theory, in relation with other areas of science.[3] However he did not only work on hard sciences, but also on philosophy, as is evident in his long correspondence with the visionary Indian spiritual thinker, Jiddu Krishnamurti.[4]

In a joint essay written in 1991, Bohm et al. describe dialogue as 'a way of exploring the roots of the many crises that face humanity today.'[5] Bohm argued that conflict, hate and irrational behaviour of all kinds have their root causes in incoherence and imbalance in our thought processes. Our thought is frequently controlled by pressures and motivations that we do not understand or recognise. Further, modern societies idolise literal thought to the neglect of 'participatory thought'.[6] Essentially, our thought is focused on classifying and distinguishing different things, individuals and groups, with little sense of their interconnection. The way we think leads to fragmentation.

Bohm held that our assumptions about thinking need to change if we are to address the lack of balance which threatens humankind and its future, namely

---

1   William Keepin, 'Lifework of David Bohm,' *ReVision*, Summer 1993, 2.

2   William Keepin, 'Lifework of David Bohm,' 2.

3   William Keepin, 'Lifework of David Bohm,' 3.

4   Keepin, William, 'Lifework of David Bohm,' 3.

5   David Bohm, Donald Factor and Peter Garrett, 'Dialogue- A Proposal,' 1991. Available on the Encyclopaedia of Informal Education website, accessed 26th December, 2012, http://www.infed.org/archives/e-texts/bohm_dialogue.htm.

6   Bohm, *On Dialogue* (Routledge, 2004), 97. For discussion of participatory thought see below.

the imbalanced relationships between people and nature and between nations and communities. By exploring ideas together in a dialogic process we can reach a greater understanding of how our thought processes lead to division or harmony, as well as gaining a greater understanding of the common challenges we face. To elucidate and address his concerns and his ideas about holistic thinking and participatory thought, Bohm developed his own comprehensive theory of dialogue, and later put his ideas on dialogue into practice.

Bohm believed that if humankind could arrive at a holistic way of understanding life and learn to think and act harmoniously, then the negative aspects of human nature could be transformed and all would be able to work for the benefit of society and humanity as a whole.[7]

7   Jim Belderis, 'David Bohm, Compassion and Understanding,' *Sunrise Magazine,* August/ September 1997, accessed 26th December, 2012, http://www.theosophy-nw.org/theosnw/ science/sc-jbel.htm.

Thought on Dialogue

Bohm defines dialogue as 'a stream of meaning flowing among and through us and between us.'[8] Such dialogue and ordinary discussion have very different characteristics. For Bohm, the main difference between dialogue and discussion is that in much ordinary discussion the participants have fixed positions and they present their own views and try to convince others to change their perspective.[9] This approach often creates tension, confrontation and distrust among the participants. These features are all harmful to the dialogic process, hindering a 'free play of thought' among the discussants. The dynamics of such a discussion obstruct the participants' ability to think creatively.[10]

In Bohm's conception of dialogue, dialogue is decidedly not about a group of people saying the same things over and over again, forever stating and restating their own position. It is not about proving one's own superiority or that of the group to which one belongs. It is not about being reactive. Bohm holds that '[i]f we defend opinions in this way [reactively], we are not going to be able to have a dialogue'; vigorously defending one's own views in order to drown out the dissenting voices of other participants does not constitute dialogue. It is natural to have presumptions and prejudices. People engaged in dialogue may come from different cultural backgrounds and have different ways of thinking. People with divergent perspectives frequently voice their assumptions and prejudices in a reactive way.[11] Often participants find themselves in a position in which '[they] just feel that something is so true... [they] cannot avoid trying to convince this stupid person how wrong he is to disagree with us.'[12]

In his comments on dialogue, Bohm has a particular model in mind, which he himself put into practice. In Bohm's conception of dialogue, a group of people engage in a free-flowing conversation in which all try hard to suspend their assumptions and listen to one another with open minds. They pay attention to their own thought processes, including their feelings and reactions, learning together about how we think and how our thought processes can be destructive or creative. Bohm suggests working with a group of between twenty and forty people seated in a single circle so that they can see and communicate with one another comfortably. This group size is large enough to encompass the diversity needed for an illuminating dialogue to develop, but not so large as to be unwieldy. Since a dialogue needs some time to get going, two hours is an ideal session length. There is no set topic for the dialogue;

---

8   Bohm, *On Dialogue*, 7.
9   Bohm, *The Essential David Bohm* (London: Routledge, 2003), 295.
10   Bohm, *The Essential David Bohm*, 295.
11   Bohm, *The Essential David Bohm*, 307.
12   Bohm, *The Essential David Bohm*, 307.

the participants should allow the dialogue to evolve naturally. Facilitators will be needed at first to help people realise the subtle differences between dialogue and other forms of group process, but they should only provide guidance for as long as it is needed, and should do so unobtrusively. Participants should be briefed about what Bohm dialogue involves before attempting it.

In engaging with dialogue, people must respect each other's viewpoints and should not resort to aggressive confrontation when disagreements arise. In the course of Bohm dialogue, each participant should be able to explore viewpoints that differ from his or her own, which leads to the acknowledgment of the 'multiple points of view' within the group without the anger and tension that are harmful to the process of dialogue.[13]

In *On Dialogue*, Bohm presents a 'vision of dialogue'.[14] Bohm defines this 'vision of dialogue' and identifies it with group thinking, or the ability to think together in unison. In dialogue in the Bohmian sense, people should be able to internalise 'other people's thought' as if it were their own thought[15] - to take part in the group's thinking. Participation includes partaking together not only in thoughts, but in the feelings and emotions present in the group as well. As Bohm states, 'when an emotional charge comes up, you share all the emotional charges, too, if they affect you; you hold them together with all the thoughts.'[16] He describes the process of thinking together as follows:

> Sometimes you may find that you are about to raise a question, but someone else brings it up. In such a case, that thought is probably latent in the group as a whole, implicit. And one person may say it, or somebody else may say it. Then another person may pick it up and carry it along. If the group is really working, that would be thinking together – common participation – as if it were all one process. That one thought is being formed together. Then, if somebody comes up with another assumption, we all listen to that, we share that meaning.[17]

As they fall into the habit of thinking together, participants in dialogue should be able to overcome impulses of irritation and hatred and establish an impersonal bond of trust and fellowship. This 'impersonal friendship' between dialogue participants is part of Bohm's 'vision of dialogue'. A sense of comradeship and trust can be

---

13   Bohm, *On Dialogue*, ix.

14   Bohm, *On Dialogue*, 36-48.

15   Bohm, *On Dialogue*, 45.

16   Bohm, *On Dialogue*, 45.

17   Bohm, *On Dialogue*, 45.

created through 'mutual participation' in the creative process of dialogue, just as it arises among football supporters standing together to watch the progress of their team.[18]

Dialogue in Bohm's sense is an attitude as well as a mechanism that lets meaning and understanding emerge. Dialogue 'can be among any number of people... Even one person can have a sense of dialogue within himself, if the spirit of the dialogue is present.'[19] It is a creative process that 'make[s] possible a flow of meaning in the whole group, out of which may emerge a new understanding. It's something new, which may not have been in the starting point at all. It's something creative. And this shared meaning is the "glue" or "cement" that holds people and societies together.'[20] Bohm argues that if the shared meaning that is the cement of a society is weak, that society will stop functioning properly.[21] Thus, in order to avoid disintegrating and falling apart, a society needs dialogue and the shared meaning that arises from it. Dialogue is essential if 'society is to cohere'.[22]

Dialogue helps us to explore the relationship between two kinds of thinking, and to redress the balance between them. In Bohm dialogue, participants reach a common consciousness, thinking together. Their thinking becomes more 'participatory'. 'Participatory thinking' is rather different to the 'literal thinking' which predominates in modern societies. Literal thought 'aims at being a reflection of reality *as it is*.'[23] The thinker is highly aware of the distinctions between different objects and persons and of their properties and uses. In participatory thought, the thinker is very aware of the interconnections between things and individuals. He has a sense of being part of a deeply connected social group, of a collective thought process, or of nature. He is aware of partaking of a larger whole, in the sense of receiving from and of contributing to it.[24] Participatory thought 'sees that everything partakes of everything.'[25] Literal thought tends to be seen as 'the best kind of thought' in much of the modern world. Bohm points out, however, that '[p]articipation is absolutely necessary if anything is to be done collectively.'[26]

---

18   Bohm, *On Dialogue*, 37.

19   Bohm, *On Dialogue*, 7.

20   Bohm, *On Dialogue*, 33.

21   Bohm, *On Dialogue*, 33.

22   Bohm, *On Dialogue*, 45.

23   Bohm, *On Dialogue*, 97.

24   Bohm, *On Dialogue*, 98.

25   Bohm, *On Dialogue*, 99.

26   Bohm, *On Dialogue*, 97, 101.

Not only did Bohm develop a theory of dialogue and arrange dialogue sessions on his own model; he also engaged in dialogue with some of the leading philosophers and spiritual leaders of his time, such as Jiddu Krishnamurti and the Dalai Lama. He engaged with these leading personalities for the sake of inspiration and exchange of ideas. In developing his theory of dialogue he drew on Krishnamurti's ideas about existence, interpersonal relations and the relationship between the observer and the observed.[27]

On several occasions in *On Dialogue*, Bohm refers to Krishnamurti's ideas and philosophy. At one point, he introduces Krishnamurti's idea that '"to be" is to be related', citing the notion that our very existence is sufficient evidence that we are all connected by a common thread.[28] In another place Bohm describes how participants should try to have an empty space before a dialogue, without obligations to do or achieve anything specific. They can then fill and then empty the space, as 'we are not trying to accumulate anything.'[29] To demonstrate this, Bohm refers to Krishnamurti's saying that 'the cup has to be empty to hold something,' a maxim that is also recounted as a Zen koan[30] in Buddhism. Finally, Bohm uses Krishnamurti's words, 'the observer is the observed,' when explaining the intimate interrelation that may exist between an observer and the thing they are observing. The distinction between the two can be blurred when a person observes another person; the observer's assumptions, the habitual opinions and convictions which shape her observation, affect the person who is being observed. The emotional response of that person in turn affects the observer and her perception of the other. Again, when a person observes her own emotions, those emotions are affected by her assumptions. The distinction between the observer and the observed is lost.

Bohm's idea that our way of thinking is the main reason the world is experiencing disorder and chaos in general is influenced by Jiddu Krishnamurti's philosophy. Bohm discusses his dialogues with Krishnamurti in one of his essays, and explains that his thoughts about why people's thinking processes must change have come about as a result of those dialogues. Bohm elucidates what he describes as Krishnamurti's 'major discovery': 'What he [Krishnamurti] was seriously proposing is that all this disorder, which is the root cause of such widespread sorrow and misery, and which prevents human beings from properly working together, has its

---

27   'Introduction to the Teachings of Jiddu Krishnamurti,' Thought Knowledge Perception Institute, accessed 26th December, 2012, http://tkpi.org/people/an-introduction-to-the-teachings-of-jiddu-krishnamurti/#.

28   Bohm, *On Dialogue*, 47.

29   Bohm, *On Dialogue*, 19.

30   A 'koan' is a parable, dialogue, or a question with a philosophical and spiritual meaning in the Zen or Chan tradition of Mahayana Buddhism.

root in the fact that we are ignorant of the general nature of our own processes of thought... [I]t may be said that we do not see what is actually happening, when we are engaged in the activity of thinking.'[31] This insight is reflected in Bohm's own emphasis on the 'proprioception' of thought in his theory of dialogue, that is, people's observations of their own thought processes. Rather than focusing on solving material problems, Bohm argued for an emphasis on the thought process itself in his dialogue groups.

Bohm also engaged in dialogue with the Dalai Lama on numerous occasions. They discussed spiritual issues and ideas pertaining to the interconnectedness of all sentient beings.[32] In an interview Bohm argues that there are parallels between the Buddhist concept of interconnectedness and his own concept of 'the implicate order', i.e. the notion that everything is related by a common thread and is an integral part of a larger reality, and that 'everything enfolds everything.'[33] Bohm adds that his dialogues with the Dalai Lama showed him these striking parallels and made him realise that there is a commonality between what he learned from Krishnamurti, the Dalai Lama, and also the teachings of Shakyamuni Buddha. Bohm notes, though, that his dialogue with Krishnamurti left a deeper impact on his dialogue philosophy because his association with the Indian thinker was much longer, lasting until Krishnamurti passed away.[34] One important point that Bohm makes regarding his dialogues with Krishnamurti and the Dalai Lama is that it is very significant to be able to think beyond our own area and tradition, instead of 'over-focus[ing] and limit[ing] everyone in [our] own little area.'[35]

Bohm had very high hopes of what his form of dialogue might achieve. One of the goals of Bohm dialogue is to solve societal problems. However, Bohm envisages this happening through a process in which we transform our fragmentary thought processes, and work towards shared meaning. Bohm argues that 'love will go away if we cannot communicate', and that if we can communicate, then 'we will have fellowship, participation, friendship, and love, growing and growing.'[36] At the end of *On Dialogue*, Bohm concludes that 'there is the possibility of the transformation of consciousness, both individually and collectively' and that this can be made possible through 'dialogue, the ability to participate in communication.'[37]

---

31   'Introduction to the Teachings of Jiddu Krishnamurti.'

32   Bohm, *On Creativity* 2nd ed (London: Routledge, 2004), 132.

33   Bohm, *On Creativity*, 133; 135.

34   Bohm, *On Creativity*, 133.

35   Bohm, *On Creativity*, 133.

36   Bohm, *On Dialogue*, 54.

37   Bohm, *On Dialogue*, 104.

Theory and Practice

Bohm did not only theorise about dialogue, but also organised dialogue groups, putting his ideas into practice. His deeply thought out, tried and tested theory of dialogue has had, and is having, an impact. It is put into practice in its original form by various groups, as well as influencing the practice of charities engaged in community building or peace-building, and influencing thought on communication in businesses and other organisations. Dialogue groups that practise Bohm dialogue precisely still function in the UK and the United States. One such group, the Marine Dialogue Group, advertise their Bohm dialogue sessions on the homepage of CGL, the Center for Group Learning, based in the San Fransisco Bay area. The Marine Dialogue Group requires participants to read Bohm's *On Dialogue* to have a sense of Bohm's understanding of dialogue before attending the sessions.[38] With a core group of twelve people, the group emphasises that they focus on 'collective thought'.[39] In line with Bohm dialogue, they do not concentrate on 'applications, social problems, [and] the news' in their sessions; they do not deal with a particular topic or pressing issue. Rather, sessions are described as 'an exploration of thought arising - what Bohm calls proprioception - and the deep examination of assumptions.'[40] An application of Bohm dialogue from the UK sees Bohm's model adapted to the internet, through the creation of a mailing list. Called the 'Dialogue List', the mailing list is described by Plymouth University lecturer Dr Paul Filmore as an 'experiment' in Bohm dialogue in cyberspace, with two main goals of 'allow[ing] participants to experience dialogue,' and creating a space to 'discuss dialogue'.[41]

One of the present authors attended a Bohm dialogue event held at St Ethelburga's Centre for Reconciliation and Peace in February 2011.[42] Even within a group of people largely new to this dialogue model, the experience was powerful. The principles of Bohm dialogue were explained at the start of the session but after the beginning of the dialogue there was almost no facilitation. The dialogue began with conversation about the process of dialogue itself, and participants' feelings about it and reactions to it. The topic seemed unimportant. What was valuable was that as

---

38   'Dialogue opportunities,' CGL (Center for Group Learning), accessed 26th December, 2012, http://cgl.org/index.html.

39   'Dialogue opportunities.'

40   'Dialogue opportunities.'

41   'Dialogue,' website of Dr Paul Filmore, accessed 26th December, 2012, http://www.tech. plym.ac.uk/dcee/staff/paulfilmoredialogue/dialogue.htm.

42   'Bohmian Dialogue: an introduction,' St Ethelburga's Centre for Reconciliation and Peace, accessed 13th February, 2013, http://www.stethelburgas.org/civicrm/event/info?id=255&reset=1.

the dialogue continued we genuinely seemed to begin to think together in a new way, following the flow of thoughts around the room. We had been asked at the start to try to take a step back and observe the thoughts and feelings arising in ourselves in response to what others said. By concentrating on this task we seemed to achieve a certain detachment from our own assumptions and emotions. In this state of relative freedom from habitual self-centred preoccupations, we seemed more able to develop ideas collaboratively. At the same time, a real sense of acceptance, trust and good will developed between the participants. For us, this experience supports Bohm's claims that this kind of dialogue has the potential to lead to creative group thinking as well as a valuable 'impersonal fellowship'.

At the same time, reflection on the experience highlighted certain limitations of the process. It demands, we feel, a considerable level of self-assurance to engage in such a dialogue, where there are no limits placed upon topics of conversation and participants are invited to explore and comment on their own reactions and emotions. It also requires a readiness to adopt a certain distance from one's own convictions. For these reasons, many people, including perhaps some people with strong attachment to religious beliefs, might have reservations about the process. Further, given the lack of particular topic, it will probably appeal chiefly to those with a particular interest in dialogue per se. This is not to say that Bohm dialogue does not have great value, or that it would not work in a religiously diverse group, only that in its pure form it may not have a very broad appeal. Nevertheless, it is an exciting process to try where groups feel comfortable with it.

Elements of it can also be adopted in the context of different dialogue models. The Conversation Café model adapts Bohm's model to provide a practical way of starting meaningful dialogue among strangers. Conversation Cafés are 'drop-in' sessions in a public place, in which a diverse group of people get together to talk about their emotions, ideas and actions, focusing on a particular theme.[43] The model can also be applied in professional contexts to enable people to 'make meaning together', to disrupt the imbalanced relationship between a 'presenter' and an 'audience', and to help people 'explore a key idea'.[44] The conversation proceeds in stages; initially participants pass round a 'talking object' and take turns in saying something about the topic in hand. After two rounds with the talking object the group moves on to 'open, spirited conversation', reminiscent of Bohm's unrestricted dialogue.[45] The agreements that the group is asked to consent to reflect Bohm's

---

43   Holman, Peggy, and Tom Devane. *The Change Handbook: Group Methods for Shaping the Future* (San Francisco: Berrett-Koehler Publishers, 1999), 349.

44   Holman and Devane. *The Change Handbook*, 350.

45   'Quick How To,' conversationcafe.org, accessed 13th Februay, 2013, http://www.conversationcafe.org/hostQuickHowTo.htm.

influence on the model; they include the following: 'Question assumptions, look for new insights' and 'suspend judgment as best you can.'[46]

Bohm's dialogic model has inspired a range of thinkers who have taken up and adapted his ideas. Peter Senge and Patricia Shaw both draw on Bohm's thought in their work on organisational change.[47] Something of the Bohmian ethos of openness and 'thinking together' is also reflected in Parker Palmer's work with dialogue for personal development.[48]

William Isaacs' understanding of dialogue is grounded in Bohm's. He incorporates Bohm's model into his step-by-step approach to participatory thinking.[49] As in the Conversation Café model, in Isaacs' process dialogue participants gradually build up to a kind of unrestricted dialogue resembling Bohm's. Each new stage brings a shift in perspective and a development in the way in which participants interact. At the first stage they simply talk to each other in what Isaacs calls 'shared monologues'. The third stage, 'reflective dialogue', is based on Bohm dialogue. There is no set topic, allowing for a free flow of thought between the participants.[50] By this stage they are learning to truly 'think together', 'in the sense of occupying a collective sensibility, in which the thoughts, emotions, and resulting actions belong not to one individual, but to all of them together.'[51]

---

46   'Quick How To.'

47   Peter M. Senge, *The fifth discipline: the art and practice of the learning organization*, (New York: Doubleday, 2006); Patricia Shaw, *Changing Conversations in Organizations*, (London: Routledge, 2002).

48   Parker J. Palmer, *A Hidden Wholeness: The Journey Toward an Undivided Life*, (San Francisco: Jossey-Bass, 2004).

49   William Isaacs, *Dialogue: the Art of Thinking Together* (Crown Publishing Group, New York, 1999), 242.

50   Isaacs, *Dialogue*, 242-290.

51   William Isaacs, 'Team Learning' in *The Fifth Discipline Fieldbook: Strategies and Tools for Building a Learning Organization*, ed. P. Senge, A. Kleiner, C. Roberts, R. B. Ross, B. J. Smith, (New York: Doubleday, 1994), 358.

Questions for Reflection

1. Have you experienced 'thinking together', in which the ideas and questions of a group seem to merge into one process of creative thinking? In your experience, what kind of environment and what kind of group allows that kind of group thinking process to take place?

2. 'Even one person can have a sense of dialogue within himself, if the spirit of the dialogue is present.'[52]

   a. What does it mean to have a sense of dialogue within yourself?

3. Bohm cites Krishnamurti's saying that 'the cup has to be empty to hold something.' Likewise, Bohm considers that dialogue participants must start with an empty space.

   a. What does it mean to start with an empty space?

   b. How could someone organising a Bohm dialogue help participants to start with an empty space?

4. How would you promote a Bohm dialogue session to attract people not already interested in dialogue processes?

5. Bohm sees great value in the kind of dialogue he proposes; it can take us to the root of all kinds of contemporary problems and can cultivate the shared understanding on which societies depend. However, to have a substantial effect on the thinking and cohesiveness of a society, some version of Bohm dialogue would presumably have to be practised far more widely than has so far been the case. How, and in what form, might Bohm dialogue reach a wider public?

---

52   Bohm, *On Dialogue*, 7.

Bibliography

Bohm, David. *On Creativity.* 2nd ed. London: Routledge, 2004.

Bohm, David. *On Dialogue.* London: Routledge, 2004.

Bohm, David. *The Essential David Bohm.* London: Routledge, 2003.

Bohm, David, Donald Factor and Peter Garrett. 'Dialogue- A Proposal.' 1991. Available on the Encyclopaedia of Informal Education website, accessed 26th December, 2012, http://www.infed.org/archives/e-texts/bohm_dialogue.htm.

CGL (Centre for Group Learning). Accessed 26th December, 2012. http://www.cgl.org/index.html.

Isaacs, William. *Dialogue: the Art of Thinking Together.* New York: Crown Publishing Group, 1999.

Isaacs, William. 'Team Learning.' In *The Fifth Discipline Fieldbook: Strategies and Tools for Building a Learning Organization,* edited by P. Senge, A. Kleiner, C. Roberts, R. B. Ross, B. J. Smith, 357-444. New York: Doubleday, 1994.

Palmer, Parker J. *A Hidden Wholeness: The Journey Toward an Undivided Life.* San Francisco: Jossey-Bass, 2004.

Senge, Peter M. *The fifth discipline: the art and practice of the learning organization.* New York: Doubleday, 2006.

Shaw, Patricia. *Changing Conversations in Organizations.* London: Routledge, 2002.

St Ethelburga's Centre for Reconciliation and Peace. 'Bohm Dialogue – an introduction.' Accessed 13th February, 2013. http://www.stethelburgas.org/civicrm/event/info?id=255&reset=1.

Thought Knowledge Perception Institute. 'Bohm with Dalai Lama.' Accessed 26th December, 2012. http://tkpi.org/people/art-science-spirituality-david-bohm-dalai-lama/.

Thought Knowledge Perception Institute. 'Introduction to the Teachings of Jiddu Krishnamurti.' Accessed 26th December, 2012. http://tkpi.org/people/an-introduction-to-the-teachings-of-jiddu-krishnamurti/#.

Recommended Reading

Bohm's Works:

Bohm, David. *On Dialogue.* London: Routledge, 2004.

Bohm, David. *The Essential David Bohm.* London: Routledge, 2003.

Bohm, David, Donald Factor and Peter Garrett. 'Dialogue- A Proposal.' 1991. Available on the Encyclopaedia of Informal Education website, accessed 26th December, 2012, http://www.infed.org/archives/e-texts/bohm_dialogue.htm.

Commentary:

Belderis, Jim. 'David Bohm, Compassion and Understanding.' *Sunrise Magazine,* August/September 1997. Available on the Theosophy North West website, accessed 5th March, 2013, http://www.theosophy-nw.org/theosnw/science/sc-jbel.htm.

Bohm Dialogue. Accessed 26th December, 2012. http://www.david-bohm.net/dialogue/.

Nichol, Lee. 'Wholeness Regained.' Kinfonet, February 2001. Accessed 5th March, 2013. http://www.kinfonet.org/articles/18-wholeness-regained---revisiting-bohms-dialogue.

Nichol, Lee. 'Wholeness Regained.' In *Dialogue as a Means of Collective Communication,* edited by Bela H. Banathy and Patrick M Jenlink, 17-28. New York: Kluwer Academic/Plenum Publishers, 2005.

Peat, David. *Infinite Potential: the Life and Times of David Bohm.* New York: Perseus Books, 1997.

Practical Applications:

Co-Intelligence Institute, The. Accessed 6th January, 2012. http://www.co-intelligence.org/P-dialogue.html.

Holman, P & Devane,T. *The change handbook: Group methods for shaping the future.* San Francisco: Berrett-Koehler Publishers, 1999.

Isaacs, William. 'Team Learning.' In *The Fifth Discipline Fieldbook: Strategies and Tools for Building a Learning Organization,* edited by P. Senge, A. Kleiner, C. Roberts, R. B. Ross, B. J. Smith, 357-444. New York: Doubleday, 1994.

Isaacs, William. *Dialogue and the Art of Thinking Together.* New York: Bantam Doubleday Dell, 1999.

Kelly, Ute and Lisa Cumming. *Civil Society Supporting Dialogue and Deliberation.* Carnegie UK Trust, 2010. Available on the Bradford University website, accessed 20th March, 2013, http://www.brad.ac.uk/ssis/media/SSIS/Documents/Civil_society_supporting_dialogue_and_Deliberation.pdf.

Palmer, Parker J. *A Hidden Wholeness: The Journey Toward an Undivided Life.* San Francisco: Jossey-Bass, 2004.

Senge, Peter M. *The fifth discipline: the art and practice of the learning organization.* New York: Doubleday, 2006.

Shaw, Patricia. *Changing Conversations in Organizations.* London: Routledge, 2002.

Martin Buber

Biographical Introduction

For the Jewish intellectual Martin Buber, 'dialogue' is a way of being and of relating to others. His sense of dialogue as a fundamental element of all worthwhile human life permeates all his mature work. According to many of his acquaintances, it also suffused his personality and life with an arresting quality of responsiveness and integrity. One described him as follows: 'This little, old man with the penetrating, incorruptible eyes… is a living proof of what this life is capable of when it wills to fulfil itself fearlessly and only in responsibility.'[1]

Buber's work and thought are not easy to categorise. Faced with the question of whether he was a theologian, a philosopher, or belonged to a different field, he described himself as 'atypical'.[2] Over a long, illustrious career he wrote and translated works on subjects ranging from religion and mythology to education, psychology and art. The influence of his work endures to this day. Indeed, one recent commentator notes that his thought has 'become ever more central to discourses in philosophy, social science, psychiatry, and education.'[3]

He was born in Vienna in 1878 into an observant Jewish family. His father had studied Darwin, while his grandfather was a prominent defender of the Jewish enlightenment, the *haskalah*. Through his grandparents Buber encountered another Jewish movement, Hasidism, which captured his imagination. Incorporating folk traditions, mysticism and the leadership of charismatic holy men or *Zaddikim*, it showed Buber a way of living in which ordinary daily activities became acts of devotion, infusing the whole of life with spiritual significance.[4] This example had a profound effect on Buber's vision of the true religious life. He produced a number of important translations and interpretations of Hasidic tales. However, as a young man he decided to pursue secular studies in philosophy and art history. He went on to work as a writer and editor before moving into academia when he was offered a post at the University of Frankfurt in 1923.

---

1   The socialist thinker Heinz-Joachim Heydorn cited in Maurice S. Friedman, *Martin Buber: the Life of Dialogue* (Chicago: Chicago University Press, 1955), 6.

2   Werner Manheim, *Martin Buber* (New York: Twayne Publishers, Inc., 1974), 10.

3   Shmuel N. Eisenstadt, 'Martin Buber in the Postmodern Age,' in *Martin Buber: a Contemporary Perspective,* ed. Paul Mendes-Flor (Syracuse: Syracuse University Press, 2002), 174.

4   Manheim, *Martin Buber,* 65.

As a young man, Buber had become actively engaged in Zionism. However, he soon became critical of the form of Zionism which focused on seeking a political solution to the threat of anti-Semitism across Europe. Buber's main concern was the need for Jewish spiritual and cultural renewal. He founded a Jewish publishing house and a periodical to this end.[5] He envisaged peaceful coexistence and collaboration between the Jews and Arabs of the Middle East. After leaving his post at Frankfurt in protest when Hitler came to power, he moved to Jerusalem. He worked as a professor at the university and founded an adult education institution training teachers to assist the integration of Jewish immigrants.

During his life Buber witnessed two world wars and the Nazi attempt to exterminate his people, as well as the early years of conflict between Arabs and Jews in the Middle East. He perceived a great and ongoing struggle between 'the human spirit' and the 'subhuman and antihuman' in human affairs, as the human spirit battled for 'the becoming of one humanity'.[6] Dialogue, he considered, precludes war. When two groups in conflict truly engage through language, they see that killing is no solution to their problem.

---

5   Asher D. Biemann, *The Martin Buber Reader* (New York: Palgrave Macmillan, 2002), 5.

6   Friedman, *Martin Buber: the Life of Dialogue*, 9.

Thought on Dialogue

In order to consider Buber's thought on dialogue we need to empty our minds of some of the more common usages of the word. Dialogue, in Buber's terms, is not just talk. Two people can talk for hours without any dialogue happening. It is not about finding out or conveying information. It is not even a particular kind of conversation. Indeed, he says that it can perfectly well occur in silence.[7]

Dialogue, for Buber, is relationship. It is a particular way or mode of being in relation to others. Human beings can relate to others in two basic modes: the 'I-It' mode and the 'I-You' mode. When people relate to one another in the I-You mode they engage in what Buber considers to be real dialogue.[8]

In this section we will explore Buber's understanding of 'dialogue', looking at the contrasts he draws between the I-You mode of being and the I-It mode. We will attempt to illustrate Buber's distinction with a story. We will note the tremendous significance of, and need for, dialogical (I-You) relationship according to Buber, and look at his assertion that real dialogue can occur between people with profoundly different outlooks. We will also briefly consider the relationship between Buber's thought on dialogue and his thought on God.

We can begin to understand the I-You mode, the mode of dialogue, by looking at the way in which Buber contrasts it with the I-It mode. When I relate to you in the I-You mode I embrace you as a whole, unique person, and I do so with my whole being. This mode is deeply personally involving; half-hearted dialogue is not, for Buber, the real thing. On the other hand, when I relate to you in the I-It mode I only relate to some of your qualities or attributes. I might notice your new hair style or your horrible shirt. I might observe that you are smiling kindly, or that something about your expression makes me uncomfortable. But whatever qualities I am responding to, I am experiencing you as a collection of qualities (for instance, 'kind', 'badly dressed', 'nice hair', 'funny expression'), not as a whole person.

In the I-You mode, I do not *experience* people or things at all. When I experience an object I am in I-It mode, exploring its qualities and gaining knowledge about it. It all happens within my mind. In the I-You mode I *encounter*. I stand in relation. The I-You mode, dialogue, involves a direct, unmediated encounter of the other in all his uniqueness. Buber states that what happens in this encounter cannot be reduced to what happens in the minds of two individuals encountering each other. While experience happens within my mind, I-You encounter happens in the realm of the '*between*': between you and me.

---

7   Martin Buber, *Between Man and Man* (London: Routledge 2002), 3f.

8   Martin Buber, *I and Thou* (New York: Simon and Schuster, 1971), 53ff. German original: *Ich und Du* (1923).

We may obtain a clearer idea of what Buber means by 'the between' by looking at his claim that in dialogue we 'experience the other side'.[9] Buber talks about the case of two people in love. Imagine that a man tenderly touches his beloved's neck. He feels with her the touch of his own hand. Buber makes it clear that it is not just a matter of him imagining the touch and feeling it on his own neck; he is somehow over there with his beloved; with her, he receives his touch in her neck.[10] In dialogue, the boundaries between separate people are somehow crossed. Without ceasing to be absolutely myself, for a moment I somehow genuinely share the other's experience.[11]

We see that, for Buber, dialogue involves a radical shift in perspective. I somehow share the perspective of the person I encounter, and he or she is suddenly right at the centre of my world. Buber writes:

> When I confront a human being as my You and speak the basic-word I-You to him, then he is no thing among things... nor... a loose bundle of named qualities. Neighbourless and seamless, he is You and fills the firmament. Not as if there were nothing but he; but everything else lives in *his* light.[12]

The encounter of two people in this mode is so direct that there is simply no room for them to put on any kind of front, or to pretend to be something they are not. Buber writes: 'No deception reaches this far; here is the cradle of actual life.'[13] Leading Buber scholar Maurice Friedman notes, 'Whatever the word "truth" may mean in other spheres, in the realm between man and man it means that one imparts oneself to the other as what one is.' This is not done by telling the other all about oneself, but by allowing him to directly 'partake of one's being.'[14] Real dialogue as defined by Buber, then, has this marvellously valuable property: it guarantees a profoundly truthful and genuine relationship for as long as it lasts.

In addition, it involves a compelling realisation of the other's significance, not in general terms of their value as a human being, but in terms of their significance *for me personally*. When I 'become aware' of someone in the I-You mode I perceive that this person, unique and whole, has something to say to me which matters for my life. In turning towards him I am accepting him, welcoming his impact on my

---

9   Buber, *Between Man and Man*, 114.

10   Buber, *Between Man and Man*, 114ff; see also 33ff.

11   See also Martin Buber, *Meetings*, ed. Maurice Friedman (La Salle, Illinois: Open Court Publishing Co., 1973), 41f.

12   Buber, *I and Thou*, 59.

13   Buber, *I and Thou*, 60.

14   Friedman, *Martin Buber: the Life of Dialogue*, 86.

life.[15] Indifference or hostility becomes impossible. Again, it is clear that dialogue as perceived by Buber is something of immense worth in interpersonal and, by extension, inter-group relationships.

Buber underlines that when I encounter somebody or something in I-You mode I am not the same as I am when I am in I-It mode. The I of the I-You mode is geared toward association with the other; it is concerned with coming together and communion. The I of the I-It mode is about differentiation; it is concerned with marking out the qualities which make people and things different and separate from one another.[16]

In dialogue, I-You encounter, I have actively to turn towards association and communion with others; I have to activate my I-You self as opposed to my I-It self. However, my action alone cannot bring dialogue about. It is an essentially reciprocal event.[17] My will and my action are necessary for me to encounter someone as a You, but the You has to be there too, confronting me. I am at once active and passive. I actively engage in dialogue, but it also happens to me, is given to me.[18] Further, it tends to be fleeting. Our natural concern to orient ourselves in our environment by dispassionately assessing our surroundings and experiences pulls us back into the world of I-It.

The unfamiliar language in which Buber talks of dialogue can sometimes make the experience he describes sound a little obscure. Yet he claims that the I-You encounter is a feature of any full human life. Looking back over our own experience may help us get to grips with what he means. Buber does *not* seem just to be talking about making an effort to see things from someone else's perspective. He is talking about something more powerful and direct.

One of the current authors associates the difference between I-It and I-You relationship with a particular incident in her relationship with a particular person. When she met Pierre he was homeless. A friend of hers had met him when he was in trouble and contemplating suicide. The friend was moving away and asked the current author to look out for Pierre. Inspired by her friend's altruism in getting involved, she wanted to help, and met Pierre regularly. They gradually got to know each other better. However, the friendship was complicated. Pierre was in a troubled situation and was not always straightforward. And the current author always saw him, to some degree, in terms of 'someone to help'. It was, for the most part, an I-It

---

15   Buber, *Between Man and Man,* 12.

16   Buber, *I and Thou,* 112.

17   Buber, *I and Thou,* 67.

18   Buber, *I and Thou,* 124.

relationship. The current author moved away but kept in touch with Pierre. Some time later he told her that he was very ill. When she next visited he was in hospital. He was completely sober, sincerely appreciative of her visit, and serious. They had no activities to distract them from the encounter and its grave circumstances. She had a new respect for this man who was facing his illness with great courage and had allowed her to see him at this time of great vulnerability. She felt as if she was seeing him for the first time. It was as if she had been watching him on a television screen, and he had stepped out of the television set and taken her hand. She felt lucky, a little awed, and rather ashamed of her previous attitude. That, she feels, was perhaps a moment of I-You encounter.

While fragile and unstable, the I-You mode is, for Buber, indispensable. It is because we can relate to others in the I-You mode, in dialogue, which gives us the status and dignity of *persons*. This is not to say that the I-It mode is wrong or evil. We need the more detached, objective I-It mode to analyse the properties of the world around us and work out how to use it for our survival and progress. It is, in any case, impossible to live in the intensity of the I-You mode all the time. However, we are not fully human, nor fully living, if we live without I-You encounter.[19]

Buber notes that, both in individuals and in societies, 'the improvement of the ability to experience and use generally involves a decrease in man's power to relate.'[20] Contemporary society's web of institutions, structures and procedures inevitably presents continual challenges to genuine dialogue. However, no environment intrinsically excludes such encounters. A simple 'sober and brotherly glance' from one worker to another in any work place can be an instance of I-You relationship.[21] The human longing for the 'actual life' of dialogical encounter is profound. In the best of human endeavours and institutions, the I-You world is allowed to pervade the I-It world, constantly interacting with and influencing it.

For those concerned with dialogue between people of different cultural, religious or social groups it may be of interest that Buber emphasises that true dialogue does not require people to be similar in any respect. Buber underlines that when I encounter someone in the I-You mode I accept him precisely as the *other*, separate and distinct from me. I allow and will him to exist in his own right as other, not just as a 'part of myself'.[22] The Canadian Christian theologian David Lochhead notes the significance of Buber's position: 'In the common sense view, [dialogue] is made possible only when the parties to dialogue have something in "common". Buber's

---

19   Buber, *I and Thou*, 85.

20   Buber, *I and Thou*, 92.

21   Buber, *Between Man and Man*, 42.

22   Buber, *Between Man and Man*, 26, 72.

understanding of the I-Thou [I-You][23] encounter does not require common ground as a precondition for dialogue.'[24]

I-You encounters can be personally deeply transformative without erasing our differences. We do not give up our different points of view. But for a moment, Buber says, we 'enter a realm where the law of the point of view no longer holds'; we are caught up in direct relation to one another.[25] Buber gives the example of his encounter with a former Christian priest. In 1914, before the First World War, the two men were at a meeting of representatives from different countries attempting to form an international authority. The Christian noted that Jews were perhaps rather overrepresented in the proposed political body, and this touched a nerve with Buber. The conversation became rather religious, with Buber making a rather provocative statement about Christians' understanding of Jesus. Both men stood up. But at that point, says Buber, 'we looked into the heart of one another's eyes... [and] before everyone we gave one another the kiss of brotherhood.'[26] Commenting on this encounter Buber says, 'The discussion of the situation between Jews and Christians had been transformed into a bond between the Christian and the Jew... Opinions were gone...' In dialogue we respond to and affirm someone in all their difference as a legitimate person. This kind of encounter can transform us, the relationship and the situation.

It is worth briefly placing Buber's thought on dialogue into the context of his thought on God. For Buber, every time we relate to a person, or indeed an animal, tree or stone in the I-You mode, we address God. God is the eternal You who, by His nature, we can never relate to as an It.[27] According to Buber's vision we meet God everywhere, in every I-You encounter. All those we meet in such encounters are signs; in responding to them we prepare ourselves for our unique work in the world and grow towards personal unity and direction.[28] There is no point withdrawing into a solitary contemplative life in search of God; He can be found wherever you are. To refuse to enter fully into relation with our fellow creatures is to refuse the encounter with God.[29]

---

23 Buber's original German term, 'Ich-du' is often translated as 'I-Thou'. We have chosen to use the more current English 'You'.

24 David Lochhead, *The Dialogical Imperative* (London: SCM Press, 1988), 50 ff. Buber's original German term, 'Ich-du' is often translated as 'I-Thou'. We have chosen to use the more current English 'You'.

25 Buber, *Between Man and Man*, 7.

26 Buber, *Between Man and Man*, 7.

27 Buber, *I and Thou*, 123.

28 Friedman, *Martin Buber: the Life of Dialogue*, 94f.

29 Buber, *I and Thou*, 127ff.

Buber tells a moving story of the incident which led him to commit to seeking God solely through dialogue with his fellow-creatures. The story underlines once again the immense worth that Buber sees in the genuine dialogue, and conveys his sense of the urgency of responding dialogically to those around us. 'In my earlier years,' he tells us, 'the "religious" was for me the exception... "Religious experience" was the experience of an otherness which did not fit into the context of life.'[30] He sought God in solitary mystical experience. One day, after Buber had spent the morning in such experience, a young man came to talk to him. Buber listened attentively and discussed matters with him, but 'without being there in spirit.' He later found out that the young man had taken his own life. Buber writes: 'I learned that he had come to me... not for a chat but for a decision. He had come to me, he had come in this hour. What do we expect when we are in despair and yet go to a man? Surely a presence by which we are told that nevertheless there is meaning.'[31] Buber considers himself to have failed the young man, by being not insufficiently wise, or insufficiently kind, but insufficiently present. The dialogue relationship of real, unmediated presence is powerful enough, he considers, to restore meaning and hope to life. It can make all the difference. The experience engendered in Buber a profound sense of responsibility, in the sense of responsiveness to the urgent claim of the other which demands our authentic presence.[32]

We have seen that for Buber dialogue is not a kind of conversation but a mode of being in relation to others. When two people meet in the I-You encounter of dialogue they perceive each other as whole persons, not as things to be understood, negotiated with or used. Dialogue as described by Buber has immense importance in human life. It can transform relationships across all kinds of divide, reconnecting people to each other and to what makes life worth living.

---

30   Buber, *Between Man and Man,* 16.

31   Buber, *Between Man and Man,* 16.

32   Buber, *Between Man and Man,* 16.

Theory and Practice

In a sense Buber himself saw practical applications for his insights everywhere, in line with his belief that any sphere of human life is barren without an element of I-You encounter. Prominent thinkers in diverse fields have shared his view, and his philosophy continues to have a significant impact on practice in a range of areas.

It is worth briefly noting Buber's considerable influence on education and psychotherapy. Buber himself applied his philosophy to education, characterising the educator as one in whom the student encounters 'the world bound up in community, turned to God', growing in constructive interaction with it.[33] Buber's dialogical notion of the teaching relationship was quickly taken up by leading educationalists and continues to inform reflections on teaching practice today.[34] Buber's thought again quickly influenced psychotherapy. In the preface to a book by one of the psychologists influenced by him, Hans Trüb, Buber emphasised the need for the psychotherapist to be ready to step outside the protection provided by his role and risk real encounter with the patient, person to person. His insights continue to be explored in this field.[35]

In the area of conflict resolution, where practitioners seek to encourage relationships in situations of conflict and distrust, Buber has again proved a valuable resource. Notably, his work influenced the approach of Dag Hammarskjöld, the second Secretary-General of the United Nations.[36]

Buber has certainly had a considerable impact on the practice of interfaith dialogue,

---

33   Buber, *Between Man and Man*, 120.

34   Maurice Friedman discusses the exploration of Buber's theory in works by Sir Fred Clarke and others: see *Martin Buber: the Life of Dialogue*, 178ff. Recent works on education referring to Buber include the following: Nel Noddings, *Caring: A Feminine Approach to Ethics and Moral Education* (Berkeley: University of California Press, 2003); Aaron Schutz, 'Caring in Schools is Not Enough: Community, Narrative, and the Limits of Alterity,' *Educational Theory* 48, no. 3 (September 1998): 373-393; Julian Stern, *The Spirit of the School* (London: Continuum, 2012).

35   For example, see: Alexandra L. Adam and Larry M. Leitner, 'Dialogical Constructivism: Martin Buber's Enduring Relevance to Psychotherapy,' *Journal of Humanistic Psychology* 51, no. 1 (January 2011): 41-60; Richard Hycner, *Between Person and Person: Toward a Dialogical Psychotherapy* (Gouldsboro: Gestalt Journal Press, 1993); Tim Kellebrew, *Brief Overview of Dialogical Psychotherapy* (TiLu Press, 2012).

36   Manuel Froehlich, *Political Ethics and the United Nations: Dag Hammarskjöld as Secretary-General* (Abingdon, Oxon: Routledge, 2008), 103ff. For a recent example of Buber's work being drawn upon in reflection on the practice of conflict resolution see Benjamin Mollov, 'Religious Diplomacy: Jewish Perspectives,' *Quarterly of Institute of International Relations (Italian Institute for the Study of International Politics)* 12 (April 2010): 69-83.

with diverse practitioners and writers highlighting the I-You relationship as an ideal of dialogue.[37] It is worth noting that Buber's thought seems to have contributed to the early development of the Catholic Church's concern with dialogue, through its 'profound influence' on Catholic theologians such as Jean Guitton prior to the Church's revolutionary Second Vatican Council.[38] [39]

Facilitators of interfaith dialogue are among the practitioners of what we might call community dialogue: those who work to bring about meaningful interaction between people of different groups (social, cultural, political and religious), outside situations of immediate conflict, with a view to increasing mutual understanding. Let us consider further what Buber has to teach practitioners in this field, which is of particular interest to us here.

The value of dialogical encounters in this context is clear. As we have seen, I-You encounters banish the dehumanising processes of prejudice and stereotyping; when they happen they involve a mutual perception of the other as a whole, unique person, acceptance of her otherness and a deep sense of her significance. We might imagine that it only remains to establish how we can make such dialogue happen.

But of course, any idea of 'making' it happen is misconceived. Many of the moments of I-You encounter that Buber describes occur spontaneously and he emphasises the elusiveness and fragility of dialogue in his terms. It cannot be forced or guaranteed. If, as dialogue practitioners, we aspire to facilitate genuine dialogue as Buber understands it, the best we can do is to put in place conditions that we think will be favourable to it, and hope.

Undoubtedly the most important conditions that facilitators might strive to put in place are internal to themselves. For the dialogue practitioner, as for the teacher and the psychotherapist, personal qualities are vital. The openness and presence of one person will often inspire the same in another. Dialogue practitioners at St Ethelburga's Centre for Reconciliation and Peace, the Interreligious Coordinating Council in Israel and the Corrymeela Community recognise this in a resource for

---

37   See, for instance, David Lochhead, *The Dialogical Imperative*; Michael Barnes, *Theology and the Dialogue of Religions* (Cambridge: Cambridge University Press, 2002); Jalees Rahman, 'Interfaith Moments,' *Harvard Divinity Bulletin* 39, nos. 3-4 (Summer/Autumn 2011).

38   The Second Vatican Council was a major conference of Catholic bishops and experts in theology which began in 1962 and concluded in 1965. Statements issued by the Council carry great authority and continue to profoundly influence the practice of the Catholic Church and its dealings with other faith groups and the world.

39   Ann Michele Nolan, *A Privileged Moment: Dialogue in the Language of the Second Vatican Council, 1962-1965* (Bern: Peter Lang, 2006), 135ff.

facilitators. They write:

> ...potentially the most important factor in good facilitation is our quality of attention. We endeavour to be fully present and attentive to the group... listening deeply to what is shared... getting to know the group members as individuals... being available between sessions for support or social contact.[40]

When this rare level of authentic presence is 'modelled' by facilitators, participants may begin to follow their example, creating more opportunities for dialogue.

For those who seek to contribute to dialogue but feel they lack the qualities of personal unity, presence and openness conducive to it, it is motivating to note Buber's theory of how these qualities are developed. A person develops them, he considers, by repeatedly risking encounter.[41] In exposing oneself to interpersonal contacts and learning to let one's guard down one can become more oriented towards the I-You world. Experience is essential for the development of quality dialogue facilitators. It might be complemented by reflection, the example of others, and training.

The dialogue relationship is, of course, not confined to the facilitated conversations which are the focus of the aforementioned resource. As one guest speaker at the Dialogue Society noted, getting together to have some fun is as promising a dialogue activity as any.[42] A relaxed, social atmosphere can help people to relate to one another. Dialogue Society workshops and conferences always include time for participants to socialise, celebrate and explore the local area together. Sometimes the most meaningful dialogue happens over a good dinner or during a coach journey, when people relax enough to shed the formality of their academic personae and relate to one another on a personal level.

Thoughtful evaluation of dialogue activities can help to progressively clear away some of the human obstacles to dialogue which we inevitably encounter, although, of course, real dialogue can never be guaranteed. Jalees Rehman recounts how he noticed at an interfaith dinner organised by his local *masjid* that people tended to speak not as individuals but as conscious representatives of their particular faiths;

---

40 'Principles of Group Facilitation,' St Ethelburga's Centre for Reconciliation and Peace, accessed 13ᵗʰ April, 2012, http://stethelburgas.org/sites/default/files/Principles of Group Facilitation_0.pdf.

41 Friedman, *Martin Buber: the Life of Dialogue,* 95ff.

42 Dialogue Society, *Making Dialogue Effective* (London: Dialogue Society, 2013), 15. Available on the Dialogue Society website, http://www.dialoguesociety.org/publications/ Making-Dialogue-Effective.pdf.
     The guest speaker mentioned was storyteller Sarah Perceval.

while the conversation was pleasant there was little genuine dialogue. At a later event he sought to allow real I-You encounters to occur by creating a 'personalized atmosphere', with people conversing in small groups. However, while moderating his group he found himself once again playing a role, and again noted the absence of real dialogue. Even concentrating too hard on facilitating well can, it seems, undermine dialogue. Nevertheless, to Rehman's delight he later met a fellow volunteer, glowing with happiness, who recounted the joyful experience of her real encounter with an elderly Protestant gentleman.[43]

It is worth evaluating events and looking for creative ways to make situations more conducive to real encounter. While Rehman's 'personalized atmosphere' initiative did not work for him, it made a space for dialogue for his fellow volunteer and the Protestant guest. Above all, it is worth simply carrying on making spaces in which dialogue may happen. As Rehman aptly concludes, 'We cannot demand or expect authentic dialogue during [for example,] interfaith events. What we can do is try to create opportunities for the transforming... moments to occur.'[44]

---

43   Jalees Rehman, 'Interfaith Moments,' *Harvard Divinity Bulletin* 39, nos. 3-4 (Summer/ Autumn 2011).

44   Jalees Rehman, 'Interfaith Moments.'

Questions for Reflection

1. Do you have experience of 'I-You' encounters:

   a. In your personal/family life?

   b. In your work?

   c. In your relations with people of different religions/belief/culture?

2. Buber says that 'all actual life is encounter'[45]. How can a person become more open to this kind of encounter?

3. David Lochhead says: 'Buber's understanding of I-Thou [I-You] encounter does not require common ground as a precondition for dialogue.'

   a. How far can dialogue go without common ground?

   b. Are there limits to it?

   c. If so, what are they?

   d. Is there any kind of common ground that we just can't do without?

4. What needs to be done to 'create opportunities for… transforming… moments to occur'[46]?

5. How applicable can Buber's approach to dialogue be to relations between groups in a socio-political context?

6. How far can Buber's thinking be applicable without its original theological grounding?

---

45   Buber, *I and Thou*, 62.

46   Rehman, 'Interfaith Moments.'

Bibliography

Adam, Alexandra L. and Larry M. Leitner. 'Dialogical Constructivism: Martin Buber's Enduring Relevance to Psychotherapy.' *Journal of Humanistic Psychology* 51 (January 2011): 41-60.

Barnes, Michael. *Theology and the Dialogue of Religions.* Cambridge: Cambridge University Press, 2002.

Biemann, Asher D. *The Martin Buber Reader.* New York: Palgrave Macmillan, 2002.

Buber, Martin. *Between Man and Man.* London: Routledge, 2002.

Buber, Martin. *I and Thou.* New York: Simon and Schuster, 1971.

Buber, Martin. *Meetings.* Edited with an Introduction and Bibliography by Maurice Friedman. La Salle, Illinois: Open Court Publishing Co., 1973.

Dialogue Society. *Making Dialogue Effective.* London: Dialogue Society, 2013. Available on the Dialogue Society website, http://www.dialoguesociety.org/publications/Making-Dialogue-Effective.pdf.

Eisenstadt, Shmuel N. 'Martin Buber in the Postmodern Age: Utopia, Community and Education in the Contemporary Era.' In *Martin Buber: a Contemporary Perspective,* edited by Paul Mendes-Flor, 174-183. Syracuse: Syracuse University Press, 2002.

Friedman, Maurice S. *Martin Buber: The Life of Dialogue.* Chicago: University of Chicago Press, 1955.

Froehlich, Manuel. *Political Ethics and the United Nations: Dag Hammarskjöld as Secretary-General.* Abingdon, Oxon: Routledge, 2008.

Hycner, Richard. *Between Person and Person: Toward a Dialogical Psychotherapy.* Gouldsboro: Gestalt Journal Press, 1993.

Kellebrew, Tim. *Brief Overview of Dialogical Psychotherapy.* TiLu Press, 2012.

Lochhead, David. *The Dialogical Imperative. A Christian Reflection on Interfaith Encounter.* London: SCM Press, 1988.

Manheim, Werner. *Martin Buber.* New York: Twayne Publishers, Inc., 1974.

Mollov, Benjamin. 'Religious Diplomacy: Jewish Perspectives.' *Quarterly of Institute of International Relations (Italian Institute for the Study of International Politics)* 12 (April 2010): 69-83.

Noddings, Nel. *Caring: A Feminine Approach to Ethics and Moral Education.* Berkeley: University of California Press, 2003.

Nolan, Ann Michele. *A Privileged Moment: Dialogue in the Language of the Second Vatican Council, 1962-1965.* Bern: Peter Lang, 2006.

Rehman, Jalees. 'Interfaith Moments.' *Harvard Divinity Bulletin* 39, nos. 3-4 (Summer/Autumn 2011).

Schutz, Aaron. 'Caring in Schools is Not Enough: Community, Narrative, and the Limits of Alterity.' *Educational Theory* 48, no. 3 (September 1998): 373-393.

Stern, Julian. *The Spirit of the School.* London: Continuum, 2012.

St Ethelburga's Centre for Reconciliation and Peace. 'Principles of Group Facilitation.' Accessed 13th April, 2012. http://stethelburgas.org/sites/default/files/Principles of Group Facilitation_0.pdf

Recommended Reading

Buber's Works:

Buber, Martin. *Between Man and Man.* London: Routledge, 2002.

Buber, Martin. *I and Thou.* New York: Simon and Schuster, 1971. First published in German, *Ich und Du,* 1923.

Buber, Martin. *Meetings.* Edited with an Introduction and Bibliography by Maurice Friedman. La Salle, Illinois: Open Court Publishing Co., 1973.

Buber, Martin. *Tales of the Hasidim.* Translated by Olga Marx. New York: Schocken Books, 1961.

Buber, Martin. *Ten Rungs: Hasidic Sayings.* New York: Schocken, 1968.

Commentary:

Friedman, Maurice S. *Martin Buber: The Life of Dialogue.* Chicago: University of Chicago Press, 1955.

Lochhead, David. *The Dialogical Imperative: A Christian Reflection on Interfaith Encounter.* London: SCM Press, 1988.

Manheim, Werner. *Martin Buber.* New York: Twayne Publishers, Inc., 1974.

Practical Applications:

Arnett, Ronald C. *Communication and Community: Implications of Martin Buber's Dialogue.* Carbondale: Southern Illinois University Press, 2001.

Cissna, Kenneth N. and Rob Anderson. *Moments of Meeting: Buber, Rogers and the Potential for Public Dialogue.* Albany: SUNY Press, 2002.

Froehlich, Manuel. *Political Ethics and the United Nations: Dag Hammarskjöld as Secretary-General.* Abingdon, Oxon: Routledge, 2008.

Rehman, Jalees. 'Interfaith Moments.' *Harvard Divinity Bulletin* 39, nos. 3-4 (Summer/Autumn 2011).

Donal Carbaugh

Biographical Introduction

Donal Carbaugh is Professor of Communication at the University of Massachusetts Amherst. He holds a Samuel F. Conti Research Fellowship, the University's highest award for research, and has also been a finalist for the university's award for outstanding teaching. He has held posts at a range of universities in Europe and Asia as well as in the United States. From 2005 to 2010 he was a member of the Research Advisory Group for the Security Needs Assessment Project of the United Nations Institute for Disarmament Research.

Carbaugh was born in a farming town near Marion, Indiana, the son of a teacher who later became a biology professor. His early life coincided with the Vietnam War, which he notes had an impact on his developing interests: 'To be in a place where people were engaged in thinking globally, and how different people can get along together better, and the means for achieving that sort of world – that was part of my enduring learning and life's quest.'[1] Following an undergraduate degree in communication and anthropology at Manchester College he studied conflict at the University of Montana. He received a PhD in conflict management, cultures and communication from the University of Washington in 1984.

His main research interests are in the way communication mediates the relationship between people and places, and in different 'cultural philosophies of communication' and their interaction in intercultural encounters.[2] This second area of interest is of particular relevance to us here. By 'cultural philosophies of communication' Carbaugh means the different ideas, principles and standards of communication that exist in different cultural worlds. His work shows that it is a mistake to assume that people of different cultures have the same rules and etiquette of communication, or that the forms of communication that we value most highly will be similarly prized by everyone else.

---

1   'Alumni Profile: Carbaugh named 2011 Distinguished Alumnus,' University of Washington, accessed 9th July, 2012, http://www.com.washington.edu/alumni/notes/profiles/carbaugh.html.

2   'Donal Carbaugh [An Interview],' *Ecologue: For members of NCA EC division and friends* (2007): 1-2, available at: http://works.bepress.com/donal_carbaugh/10; 'Selected Works of Donal Carbaugh: Author Home,' Selected WorksTM, accessed 9th July, 2012, http://works.bepress.com/donal_carbaugh/.

His approach to communication studies is an ethnographic one; he focuses on exploring, recording and analysing real conversations among people of diverse cultures. His work is rich in accounts of such conversations, taken from chance incidents in his personal and professional life as well as from fieldwork. A summary of one account of intercultural (mis)communication will set the scene for our exploration of Carbaugh's work on dialogue.

Carbaugh relates a conversation between American business professors and Russian professors visiting them, in the late 1980's, to learn about free market economics.[3] After a little initial conversation the American professors asked directly how they could assist their Russian colleagues. In response, the Russians extolled the virtues of their own school. Baffled, the Americans spoke about the challenges *they* had faced in an attempt to encourage the Russians to open up. This only added to the general confusion. At the root of this miscommunication, Carbaugh explains, are conflicting cultural philosophies or sets of norms of communication. Russian norms include the principle that when speaking with outsiders, one should expound the virtues of one's country. This principle clashed with the American principle of sharing problems and challenges openly in order to find solutions together. However good the intentions of those involved, failure to appreciate the existence of different cultural philosophies of communication can lead to disaster.

---

3   Donal Carbaugh, *Cultures in Conversation,* (New York, NY: Lawrence Erlbaum and Associates, 2005), 17 ff.

Thought on Dialogue

Donal Carbaugh's approach to dialogue is somewhat different to the others explored in this book. He does not offer a model or ideal of dialogue and advise on how it might be successfully put into practice. Rather, he explores what people in different cultural contexts actually mean when they use the term 'dialogue', or equivalent terms, and examines the activities to which they are referring.

'Dialogue', Carbaugh notes, is a pervasively used, richly meaningful term in contemporary English. Passionate calls for dialogue are made in contexts ranging from academia to international relations, on issues from education to religious diversity to ethnic conflict. These calls for dialogue are underpinned by a whole system of ideas about a valued form of communication, its goals, and how it should be conducted.[4]

Carbaugh highlights in his work on dialogue that we cannot assume that all our potential dialogue partners will share our own particular understanding of dialogue, or that the kind of dialogue we propose will have universal appeal. Forms of communication, including 'dialogue', are deeply connected to culture, to 'those means and meanings of practice which each people believe, and which they value as so significant and important to them.'[5] Different peoples have different communicative practices and principles, from the Antiguan practice of animated talk by many speakers at once, to the meaningful periods of silence in conversations in central Finland. Practices and principles of communication vary with language, culture and nation, and even within languages, societies and nations. Concepts and practices of dialogue are no exception: they are shaped by cultural contexts.[6]

Carbaugh, in partnership with other scholars with different linguistic and cultural backgrounds, has explored a range of terms in different languages which share some of the meaning of the English term 'dialogue.' He identifies significant

---

4   Donal Carbaugh, David Boromisza-Habashi and Xinmei Ge, 'Dialogue in cross-cultural perspective,' in *Aspects of Intercultural Dialogue*, ed. N. Aalto and E. Reuter (Koln: SAXA Verlag, 2006), 27 f.

5   Donal Carbaugh, 'Dialogue and Multicultural Dynamics: Challenges to Hearing Cultures in Conversation,' in *Debating Multiculturalism 2: Workshop Proceedings*, ed. Steve Garner and Seref Kavak (London: Dialogue Society, 2012), 73.

6   Carbaugh suggests that Martin Buber's idea of dialogue as a direct, intense, but tragically fleeting interpersonal encounter reflects his cultural context as a Jewish intellectual in the wake of the Second World War; the horrific sufferings of Buber's people during the war presumably contributed to his sense of the fragility of human life and relationships. Carbaugh, 'Dialogue and Multicultural Dynamics: Challenges to Hearing Cultures in Conversation,' 74 f.

variation as well as important areas of common ground. We will look briefly at his methodology, consider some of the terms he explores in different languages, and explore his comparative analysis of the data.

First though, it is worth noting that the American English ideal of 'good communication' which underlies many calls for 'dialogue' must be understood as a cultural ideal, not a universal standard. This is Carbaugh's starting point. He explores this ideal as it is manifested, among other places, in the long-running American talk show, 'Donahue'.[7] 'Good communication', he explains, is a valued way of interacting which is bound up with the cultural ideals of the unique, free self, and of the coming together of unique individuals in voluntary relationships. In good communication, individuals come together to confront some kind of problem through close, supportive and flexible communication. 'Being honest' and 'sharing' are important related concepts referring to practices often involved in good communication. Being honest is an open, direct assertion of truth which is valued and often praised, sometimes even when the truth disclosed is problematic or shameful. Sharing is a disclosure of personal experience or information in a supportive way that reaffirms relational bonds.

Having established the kind of ideals and principles functioning in American English calls for 'dialogue', let us briefly look at the method that was used by Carbaugh in exploring and analysing roughly equivalent or related concepts in different languages in his studies to date.[8] The approach was an ethnographic one; that is, the analysis of terms was based on concrete examples of communication in particular cultural contexts. For each given language, the researchers identified terms with meanings which overlapped significantly with the meaning of the English word 'dialogue.' They explored exactly how the term was used in particular contexts. They examined which actual practices were being referred to by the term, considering individual acts of communication, 'events' involving the acts of more than one person, and broader styles of communication. Finally, they analysed in depth the meanings of the terms. As well as considering the terms' explicit meanings about kinds of communication practices, they turned the spotlight on the implied

7   Donal Carbaugh, *Talking American: Cultural Discourses on Donahue,* (New York: Ablex, 1988), Unit 2.

8   Carbaugh, Boromisza-Habashi and Ge, 'Dialogue in cross-cultural perspective,' 28; Carbaugh, Elena V. Nuciforo, Makoto Saito and Dong-shin Shin, '"Dialogue" in Cross-Cultural Perspective: Japanese, Korean and Russian Discourses,' *Journal of International and Intercultural Communication* 4, no. 2 (May 2011): 89 f.

messages about social relations and institutions, and about personhood.[9] The insights of native speakers informed the process.

In Japanese, Carbaugh and his colleagues found, two terms come close to the English 'dialogue': *taiwa* and *hanashiai*. While they are often treated as interchangeable in colloquial conversation, they can be differentiated: '*Hanashiai* means talking together with each side's talk matching the other. *Taiwa* means people talking about particular issues face to face. *Taiwa* is *hanashiai* in which harmony..., mutual understanding..., and mutual respect... are promoted.'[10] *Hanashiai* is a mode of communication developed during Japan's Edo period (1603-1886) as a means of achieving consensus, suitable for use even in groups of mixed social status. Carbaugh looks at *hanashiai* in action in an educational television series, *Haato wo tunagou*, (Let's Bridge Hearts), which facilitates *hanashiai* on sensitive issues. In one episode, the interactions between a young woman struggling with gender identity, the host and her parents explore verbally the kind of conversation the family might have, and also embody some of the practices and principles involved in *hanashiai*. The participants engage in three key communicative acts involved in *hanashiai*: compromise, giving advice and being self-critical. The host and the parents gently advise further discussion before the young woman makes any final decisions about her future, the young woman shows willingness to engage in these and the parents apologise for their failure to help their child in her distress. The interactions of the participants reflect a profound cultural concern to balance the concerns of the emotional self (*hone*) and the social self (*tatemae*). Respect for the emotional self grounds the acceptance of differences. Respect for the social self demands a respectful readiness to compromise, and attempts towards at least a partial consensus at the level of the social self.

In Russian диалог, pronounced *dee-a-log*, is the nearest equivalent to 'dialogue'. Carbaugh and his colleagues analyse the usage of the term since the 1950's, which incorporates meanings borrowed from English usages of 'dialogue'. In this recent usage, диалог refers to 'an interaction which brings people together in an effort to accomplish various communication acts, events, and a style of social action.'[11]

---

9   The work used a particular theoretical model which is given in Carbaugh, 'Fifty terms for talk: a cross-cultural study,' *International and Intercultural Communication Annual* 13 (1989):93-120. This model provides the analytic focus on three levels of communicative practice: acts, events and styles, and on three levels of meaning: about communicative practice, about social roles and institutions, and about personhood.

10   Carbaugh, Nuciforo, Saito and Shin, '"Dialogue" in Cross-Cultural Perspective: Japanese, Korean and Russian Discourses,' 90.

11   Carbaugh, Nuciforo, Saito and Shin, '"Dialogue" in Cross-Cultural Perspective: Japanese, Korean and Russian Discourses,' 97.

Диалог, typically, addresses some form of social or political problem. Consensus is not an essential goal but the process should contribute to mutual understanding, collaboration and partnership in addressing common challenges. The tone of диалог tends to be relatively formal and it is ordered according to particular moral norms, including the following: '(1) There must be mutual respect and consideration for all participants at all times...; (2) harsh critique of others and negative emotions must be avoided.'[12]

In Finnish, Carbaugh and his colleagues identified the word *keskustelu* as perhaps the term most closely approximating to 'dialogue.' It is often translated as 'discussion'. Another term for talk, *vuoropuhelu*, which means 'to talk together, taking turns', has become less common over the course of the last generation. A related term, *vuorovaikutus* means an 'exchange of influencing'. Carbaugh notes that 'the range of Finnish terms... brings into view the importance of the matter under discussion (i.e. *vuoropuhelu*), the interactive quality of discussion (i.e. *keskustelu*), and mutual influence (i.e., *vuorovaikutus*).' The decline in use of *vuoropuhelu* suggests a shift in communicative values, 'a movement toward interactive discussion as a code for social relations and expressive life.'[13]

Carbaugh's analysis of the use of terms approximating to 'dialogue' in Japanese, Russian, Finnish, Blackfoot, Chinese, Finnish, Hungarian and Korean ground a set of observations about the kind of meanings that are active where these terms are used. The terms describe particular valued forms of communication, involving a particular ethos, goals and practice. They also imply certain messages about social roles, within and beyond the form of communication in question, and about persons and how they should behave. Looking at the following summary, taken from one of Carbaugh's articles, we see that it highlights significant overlapping areas of meaning across terms from different cultures while also recognising and leaving space for particularity and difference.[14] Each feature below is active in some but not necessarily all cases.

A) Meanings being expressed about communication practices when 'dialogue' or a term translated as something like 'dialogue' is being used.

---

12   Carbaugh, Nuciforo, Saito and Shin, '"Dialogue" in Cross-Cultural Perspective: Japanese, Korean and Russian Discourses,' 100.

13   Carbaugh, Boromisza-Habashi and Ge, 'Dialogue in cross-cultural perspective,' 38 f.

14   This summary is taken from Carbaugh, 'Dialogue and Multicultural Dynamics: Challenges to Hearing Cultures in Conversation,' 76 ff.

These are the most literal and explicit meanings at play:

1. The terms refer to face-to-face, verbal co-productions, between two or more parties.

2. The practices being referenced range from cooperative interactions, to competitive debates.

3. An ethos of mutuality of exchange (or interdependence) pervades these practices.

4. The predominant tone or feeling is socially collaborative, and varies from serious and formal to informal.

5. The predominant channel is face-to-face conversation, but also includes writing, scripted and spontaneous practices, as well as various electronic media (newsprint, internet, radio, television).

6. Structuring norms include speaking in a sincere, informative, and ably expressive way about one's views; and listening in a way that is open to the views, and to the emotions of others.

7. Goals of the practice vary widely from producing harmony, to winning a verbal contest, to informing participants about issues, problem-solving, clarifying the nature of the issues, presenting a range of views, developing shared understanding, mutual trust, resolving a conflict in a mutually satisfying way, transforming social circumstances, establishing a common goal, affirming and/or repairing social relationships, to establishing future actions.

8. The practices of 'dialogue' are conceived to be of varying importance, but most are deemed highly efficacious, yet the locus or site of the efficacy varies: in some cases, the weightiness is in the relations among the participants (as more important than the information exchanged), in others, the weightiness is in the topic being addressed (as presumably weighty e.g., societal issues, political, economic matters); in still others, the weightiness concerns value in the form of the social activity getting done (and is not so much focused on the topic of discussion); or further, the weight is in the balance between clarity of the information expressed, the agreement being forged, and the emotion involved in its expression.

B) More implicit meanings being expressed about sociality, social relations, or social institutions... As people talk about the importance of 'dialogue,' they are also saying something about the arrangement of social identities, relations, and possibly institutions. These meanings can be formulated as follows:

1. The dialogic form of practice gives voice to various social identities: Political or social opponents; high status participants e.g., scholars, officials; guests and hosts; disputants and intermediaries; employers and employees.

2. The form presumes social relations of equality, or as moving in some senses toward equality.

3. The form can activate various social institutions: political-governmental, religious, educational, friendship, therapeutic, health, entertainment media (radio, television, theatre, opera).

4. The dialogic form is designed to balance relations among people including, within social scenes, their social and emotional self.

C) Premises these terms activate about proper conduct and personhood. As with the meanings above about sociality, these are largely taken-for-granted, and are as a result expressed more implicitly and metaphorically... These can be formulated as follows:

1. Persons can be insincere, conniving, or inappropriately inexpressive.

2. Persons can act on the basis of their own selfish interests, on the basis of an imbalance of power, or in other imbalanced ways.

3. The above are ultimately limited, immoral, or bad.

4. Persons need forms of social interaction which are sincere, informative, expressive of their views, AND, receptive to the views of others.

5. Persons need forms of social interaction which are educational (disseminate information widely) and socially productive (advance mutual interests in socially productive ways).

6. Persons need forms of social interaction which balance informational needs and social care.

7. These needs are attached to various philosophical, literary, and cultural traditions (axioms of particularity and of actuality).

What is identified here is a 'range of general features that are active when people call for dialogue.'[15] There is sufficient overlap between the meanings of terms for us to recognise practices approximating to 'dialogue' in diverse cultures. However, in

---

15   Carbaugh, Nuciforo, Saito and Shin, '"Dialogue" in Cross-Cultural Perspective: Japanese, Korean and Russian Discourses,' 104.

studying or working with these concepts and practices, it is crucial to attend to the considerable variety encompassed within this group of 'dialogue' terms. Different norms function in 'dialogue' in the different cultural systems, with different boundaries defining what activities are legitimate within the practice. Direct criticism of other participants may be unacceptable in the context of a Russian диалог but legitimate within Japanese *hanashiai* as long as it is expressed with the requisite respect and consideration. Different goals and priorities in dialogue may lead to different evaluations of a particular dialogue process by the different parties. In a diplomatic dialogue, Russian participants may judge the process's success on the levels of mutual understanding achieved, while American participants might be more focused, in this sort of dialogical context, on more concrete progress made and decisions reached. Any participant in a dialogue may be juggling a number of concerns, from achieving consensus, to ensuring a pleasant atmosphere, to presenting one's country favourably, to revealing truth. 'How one resolves the tension,' though, 'as a practical matter typically resides within one's customary ways.'[16]

Given such diversity, Carbaugh notes, 'we cannot assume different participants come to dialogue with the same context, acts, events, styles and meanings in view.' He proposes the framework used by himself and his colleagues as a means to proper understanding of the meaning of 'dialogue' for participants coming from different cultural worlds. This work, he hopes, 'will help maximise the possibilities while minimizing the pitfalls of intercultural dialogue.'[17]

---

16   Carbaugh, 'Dialogue and Multicultural Dynamics: Challenges to Hearing Cultures in Conversation,' 83.

17   Carbaugh, Nuciforo, Saito and Shin, '"Dialogue" in Cross-Cultural Perspective: Japanese, Korean and Russian Discourses,' 106.

Theory and Practice

The light shed by Carbaugh's work on the cultural variation of meanings of 'dialogue', and of philosophies of communication more generally, is of clear value to diverse practitioners dealing with intercultural interactions. In this section we will take a brief look at how some researchers are applying his methods to practical contexts involving intercultural encounters. We will then consider what practitioners of intercultural dialogue can do to negotiate the cultural variation of the meaning of 'dialogue' when detailed research is not immediately available or practicable.

A number of scholars have actively used Carbaugh's approach to the analysis of cultural communication, called 'cultural discourse analysis,' to inform work involving intercultural interaction, notably in the humanitarian sector.[18] Saskia Witteborn explores the philosophy of communication active in the work of transnational NGO (non-governmental organisation) Save the Children in Urumqi, China.[19] Interviews with staff and analysis of the organisation's website revealed clear commitment to participatory decision-making, self-expression, sharing information and transparency. Clients in China were encouraged to embrace these practices in educational projects run by the NGO. Witteborn notes that the NGO, in effect, assumes the universality of its communication values, which are actually culturally relative, grounded in a vision of global citizenship which belongs to donor countries. Observations of communication among local Chinese people showed different norms of communication reflecting different cultural values; children, for instance, are not generally encouraged to participate in significant decision-making or to talk much in class. Witteborn underlines the need for NGOs to recognise and reflect upon the way in which they import communication values, and to monitor the effect of this process on the communities they serve.

In a project for the United Nations Institute for Disarmament Research, Derek B. Miller and Lisa Rudnick are drawing on cultural discourse analysis to help actively improve the effectiveness of UN humanitarian operations relating to community security. They note that to optimise a project's impact and sustainability it must be responsive to the needs of the community as understood by community members. Their Security Needs Assessment Protocol (SNAP) is a process designed to achieve this. A specialist SNAP research team, after consultation with an agency running

---

18   Carbaugh describes his methodology, 'cultural discourse analysis', in full in 'Cultural discourse analysis: the investigation of communication practices with special attention to intercultural encounters,' *Journal of Intercultural Communication Research* 36 (2007): 167-182.

19   Saskia Witteborn, 'The role of transnational NGOs in promoting global citizenship and globalizing communication practices,' *Language and Intercultural Communication* 10, no. 4 (November 2010): 358-372.

a humanitarian project, researches the meaning of 'security' for local people using cultural discourse analysis. The SNAP team helps the agency to relate this research to their work and to find ways of enhancing that work by '[integrating] standing agency practices and goals with local systems of practice and belief.'[20] A 2007 'pre-test' of the Protocol in Ghana suggested that it has potential to yield rich cultural data that could enhance a range of humanitarian projects.

In the field of education, Carbaugh's work has made a significant contribution to improving the intercultural understanding of US academics who teach Native American students. Teaching at a university he encountered a young woman belonging to Blackfeet Indian Nation based on a reservation in northern Montana.[21] Asked to deliver a short speech during a public speaking course she was utterly dismayed, trembling and exclaiming, 'I can't do that!' Carbaugh gained a better understanding of the challenges she faced through spending time with Blackfeet people and learning about their ways. He came to see that her reaction stemmed from deep differences between Blackfeet and 'Whiteman's' philosophies of communication. The university course promoted public speaking, regardless of age or status, as a valuable means of expressing oneself and a part of citizenship. In Blackfeet traditional culture, in public, silence rather than speech is the primary mode of communication for younger people, and speaking in public is a risky activity which can potentially threaten the profound interconnections among people. Requiring experience and appropriate training, public speaking is generally undertaken by older men. Carbaugh's student was being asked to do something which conflicted painfully with the norms of her native cultural world. Carbaugh has informed teaching practice by sharing his findings about Blackfeet communication styles with colleagues through discussion, publications and conferences.

Carbaugh's findings also have implications for the designers of various democratic processes. Public consultation processes and all kinds of participatory democracy which demand that people 'speak up verbally and be heard' will inevitably exclude Blackfeet people since 'the demand itself supplants the very goal it seeks to attain.'[22] However inclusive the intention behind such processes, cultural difference may render it useless for some prospective participants. Research into cultural discourse can clearly provide important insights for agencies looking for genuinely inclusive democratic processes.

---

20   Derek B. Miller and Lisa Rudnick, *The security needs assessment protocol: improving operational effectiveness through community security* (New York and Geneva: United Nations Publications, 2008), 43.

21   Carbaugh, *Cultures in Conversation,* ch.6.

22   Carbaugh, *Cultures in Conversation*, 95. Carbaugh and Karen Wolf examine a related case in 'Situating rhetoric in cultural discourses,' *International and Intercultural Communication Annual*, 22 (1999): 19-30.

The value of such research is equally clear for those concerned with various kinds of intercultural dialogue at the community level. Where such research is available, or where carrying it out is practicable, it offers dialogue practitioners better understanding of the kinds of communication that are likely to be acceptable and appealing to target groups. There is undoubtedly space for further research in this area.

Even where we lack immediate access to research on the groups which we hope to bring together in dialogue, Carbaugh's key insights on the variation of meanings of 'dialogue' provide valuable food for thought about dialogue practice. We might be taken with a particular model for dialogue, like Bohm's or Yankelovich's perhaps, and feel baffled when others fail to engage with it. It is well worth reminding ourselves that since ideals of communication differ, one size does not fit all. Intercultural sensitivity is as important in choosing a format for dialogue as it is during the dialogue itself.

How can we go about achieving this even without access to thorough research?

Training on cultural difference in communication may help develop a general understanding of and sensitivity towards cultural difference in communication. It is something that is sometimes included in facilitation training, for instance at St Ethelburga's Centre for Reconciliation and Peace, as well as being offered by more business-focused training agencies.[23]

Training aside, preliminary meetings with a community leader from the group with whom we hope to engage may be helpful. A little conversation about what kind of intercultural interactions his or her group might appreciate, and why, can help us to be more responsive to their needs and preferences.

Flexibility, generosity and imagination might be considered key virtues in the planning of dialogue, in light of cultural variations in dialogue ideals. Dialogue organisers need to be ready to adapt or abandon models of dialogue that do not work for partner groups. It may also be fruitful to step outside our own comfort zone and embrace a form of interaction that might 'belong' to another group more than our own. Where a group's communication values are markedly different from our own it will take imagination to step outside the box and explore what forms of

---

23   http://www.stethelburgas.org. At a more comprehensive level, several UK universities now offer master's degrees in Intercultural Communication (including the University of Bedfordshire, the University of the West of England, the University of Sheffield, the University of Manchester, the University of East Anglia and Anglia Ruskin University).

interaction might be acceptable to them.[24]

Where it is difficult to find a model for dialogue that we feel will work for all participants, it may be wise to begin with modes of interaction that are not too tightly tied to particular ideals of communication. Informal shared meals or cultural activities may be a good place to start. Within such contexts people may gradually get to know each other and build the understanding and confidence to move on to deeper interactions in appropriate ways. The Dialogue Society has tended to use this approach, and the organisation's Community Dialogue Manuals provide guidance to help other groups use simple community activities as a starting point for dialogue.[25] Similarly, the Tony Blair Faith Foundation uses a 'hands, to heart, to head' approach, building initial trust and understanding for dialogue through joint social action and allowing other kinds of dialogue to grow out of this.[26] Carbaugh's work, reminding us that even 'dialogue' is culturally variable, can help guide us towards cultural sensitivity and real inclusivity in our intercultural encounters.

---

24   Carbaugh provides an example for us here in his reflections on what Blackfeet people might ask of the non-native Americans who try to involve them in deliberative democracy: 'if the Blackfeet were to make a demand, it might be for us to watch and listen, to be respectful and modest of that which we are all a part, especially when in the presence of something to which we are not yet attuned, like a deep cultural difference.' Carbaugh, *Cultures in Conversation*, 95.

25   'Community Publications,' Dialogue Society, accessed 20th March, 2013, http://www. dialoguesociety.org/publications/community.html.

26   'Faith and Development Seminar,' Tony Blair Faith Foundation, accessed 20th March, 2013, http://www.tonyblairfaithfoundation.org/news/2012/06/14-0.

Questions for Reflection

1. Carbaugh considers that the kind of ethnographic research carried out by himself and his colleagues 'help maximise the possibilities while minimizing the pitfalls of intercultural dialogue.'[27]

    a. How far can academic research assist dialogue practitioners?

    b. How far do practitioners actually draw on research?

    c. How might exchange between practitioners and researchers be improved?

2. Carbaugh's description of the meeting between Russian and American researchers, summarised in our 'Biographical Introduction', offers a good example of failed intercultural communication.

    a. Have you witnessed examples of failure and of success in intercultural communication?

    b. In your experience, what factors make for failure or success?

3. Given different understandings of dialogue in different cultural worlds, what would you do to help ensure the success of a dialogue planned between two different cultural groups?

4. Carbaugh highlights the fact that cultural philosophies of communication make it deeply problematic for some people to express themselves in public. How might organisers of dialogue in democratic or intercultural contexts ensure that these people's perspectives are taken into account, without forcing them into a problematic form of participation?

5. Saskia Witteborn's study of Save the Children's work in Urumqi shows how international agencies sometimes assume that their own philosophies of communication are universally valid. How should international agencies balance the concern to introduce practices they consider helpful with respect for intercultural difference in communication?

---

27   Carbaugh, Nuciforo, Saito and Shin, '"Dialogue" in Cross-Cultural Perspective: Japanese, Korean and Russian Discourses,' 106.

Bibliography

Carbaugh, Donal. 'Cultural discourse analysis: the investigation of communication practices with special attention to intercultural encounters.' *Journal of Intercultural Communication Research,* 36 (2007): 167-182.

Carbaugh, Donal. *Cultures in Conversation.* New York, NY: Lawrence Erlbaum and Associates, 2005.

Carbaugh, Donal. 'Dialogue and Multicultural Dynamics: Challenges to Hearing Cultures in Conversation.' *Debating Multiculturalism 2: Workshop Proceedings,* edited by Steve Garner and Seref Kavak, 71-83. London: Dialogue Society, 2012. Available on the Dialogue Society website, http://www.dialoguesociety. org/publications/debating-multiculturalism-2.pdf.

Carbaugh, Donal. 'Fifty terms for talk: a cross-cultural study.' *International and Intercultural Communication Annual,* 13 (1989): 93-120.

Carbaugh, Donal. *Talking American: Cultural Discourses on Donahue.* New York: Ablex, 1988.

Carbaugh, Donal, David Boromisza-Habashi and Xinmei Ge. 'Dialogue in cross-cultural perspective.' In *Aspects of intercultural* dialogue, edited by N. Aalto and E. Reuter, 27-46. Koln: SAXA Verlag, 2006.

Carbaugh, Donal, Elena V. Nuciforo, Makoto Saito and Dong-shin Shin. '"Dialogue" in Cross-Cultural Perspective: Japanese, Korean and Russian Discourses.' *Journal of International and Intercultural Communication* 4, no. 2 (May 2011): 87-108.

Carbaugh, Donal and Karen Wolf. 'Situating rhetoric in cultural discourses.' *International and Intercultural Communication Annual,* 22 (1999): 19-30.

Miller, Derek B. and Lisa Rudnick. *The security needs assessment protocol: improving operational effectiveness through community security.* New York and Geneva: United Nations Publications, 2008.

Witteborn, Saskia. 'The role of transnational NGOs in promoting global citizenship and globalizing communication practices.' *Language and Intercultural Communication* 10, no. 4 (November 2010): 358-372.

Recommended Reading

Carbaugh's Works:

Carbaugh, Donal. 'Cultural discourse analysis: the investigation of communication practices with special attention to intercultural encounters.' *Journal of Intercultural Communication Research,* 36 (2007): 167-182.

Carbaugh, Donal. *Cultures in Conversation.* New York, NY: Lawrence Erlbaum and Associates, 2005.

Carbaugh, Donal. 'Dialogue and Multicultural Dynamics: Challenges to Hearing Cultures in Conversation.' *Debating Multiculturalism 2: Workshop Proceedings,* edited by Steve Garner and Seref Kavak, 71-83. London: Dialogue Society, 2012. Available on the Dialogue Society website, http://www.dialoguesociety.org/publications/debating-multiculturalism-2.pdf.

Carbaugh, Donal. 'Putting Policy in its Place through Cultural Discourse Analysis.' Paper presented at the 2008 International Colloquium on Communication, Schoodic Peninsula, Maine, USA. Available on Selected Works of Donal Carbaugh website, accessed 20th March, 2013, http://works.bepress.com/donal_carbaugh/22.

Carbaugh, Donal, David Boromisza-Habashi and Xinmei Ge. 'Dialogue in cross-cultural perspective.' In *Aspects of intercultural* dialogue, edited by N. Aalto and E. Reuter, 27-46. Koln: SAXA Verlag, 2006.

Carbaugh, Donal, Elena V. Nuciforo, Makoto Saito and Dong-shin Shin. '"Dialogue" in Cross-Cultural Perspective: Japanese, Korean and Russian Discourses.' *Journal of International and Intercultural Communication* 4, no. 2 (May 2011): 87-108.

Practical Applications:

Miller, Derek B. and Lisa Rudnick. *The security needs assessment protocol: improving operational effectiveness through community security.* New York and Geneva: United Nations Publications, 2008.

Witteborn, Saskia. 'The role of transnational NGOs in promoting global citizenship and globalizing communication practices.' *Language and Intercultural Communication* 10, no. 4 (November 2010): 358-372.

Fethullah Gülen

Biographical Introduction

Muhammed Fethullah Gülen is a Turkish Muslim scholar, opinion leader and peace advocate. He is one of the world's most influential Muslim teachers, the inspiration behind a major transnational civil society movement. He was born in 1941 in the village of Korucuk, in the Erzurum province of Turkey. Between 1959 and 1981 he was a state licensed preacher. During this time and after retiring from this post Gülen travelled extensively in Turkey and abroad, addressing diverse gatherings on issues relating to faith, responsibility, modernity, science and society.

As an Islamic scholar and public intellectual, Gülen has authored over 60 books and continues to write the editorial for a number of periodicals such as *The Fountain,* a magazine of spiritual and scientific thought. His extensive learning in both religious and non-religious disciplines allows him to reach a diverse audience and to bridge-build between disparate fields. One of his on-going intellectual projects is the *Key Concepts of Sufism*, a multi-volume collection of essays explaining how Sufi concepts originate from and are rooted in the Qur'an and Sunnah.[1] He is not a 'liberal', 'modernist' or 'reformer'; he speaks from within the Sunni Hanafi tradition of Islam, offering an authentic re-reading of religion, suggesting new ways of engaging with contemporary ideas and realities. He is widely known for his pro-dialogue and pro-democracy stance, and his utter opposition to any form of terrorism.

Gülen, who topped the July 2008 Foreign Policy and Prospect magazines' poll of most influential public intellectuals, has initiated and inspired a worldwide civil society movement known by participants as Hizmet, literally 'Service', though sometimes referred to as the Gülen Movement, a term of which Gülen disapproves. Participants invest and engage in nondenominational education and intercultural dialogue projects intended to contribute towards durable peace and greater understanding. Loosely connected by shared ideals and principles, the movement is now active across the world through schools, universities, dialogue organisations and other charitable NGOs. Gülen has developed a broad readership and the movement now attracts participants from diverse backgrounds, including people of other religious faiths and none.

---

1   The Sunnah consists of the example, instructions and actions of the Prophet Muhammed.

While Gülen's exposition of Islam has always been inclusive and dialogic, it was in the early 1990s that he began particularly advocating the need for dialogue initiatives and organisations to ensure that the focus on dialogue continued throughout the year. He set an example by his visits to religious and ethnic leaders such as the Patriarch of the Turkish Orthodox community, the Patriarch of the Turkish Armenian community, the Chief Rabbi of the Turkish Jewish community, leaders of the Turkish Alevi community, Pope John Paul II and the Chief Sephardic Rabbi of Israel. Given his public standing in Turkey, these meetings helped legitimise minority communities among the wider Turkish public. Gülen was personally involved in setting up the Journalists and Writers Foundation, which continues to organise dialogue events bringing together people of opposing viewpoints and divergent lifestyles. These initiatives had a significant, nationwide impact in Turkey with reactions documented in the newspaper columns of the time.

In 2010 Gülen was awarded an honorary doctorate by Leeds Metropolitan University for his contribution to education, peace-making and intercultural dialogue. In 2011 in New York he was awarded an EWI Peace Building Award by the East West Institute for his contribution to world peace. In the same year the Senate of the US State of Texas passed a resolution commending him for his contributions to the promotion of global peace and understanding. Several university chairs have been established to study his work, the most recent being the Fethullah Gülen Chair for Intercultural Studies at KU Leuven, Belgium.

Thought on Dialogue

Gülen's conception and practice of dialogue developed through the 1970s and 80s, in the context of modern Turkey where various groups, differentiated by economic class, ideology or kind or degree of religious belonging, confronted each other in latent or open hostility. They shared a language, a land, a long history, yet they were unable to imagine any community of ideas or purposes. Gülen began to address this problem in his role as a state-licensed preacher, preaching not only in mosques but also coffee houses and other public places.

In the early 1990s Gülen encouraged those inspired by his teachings to organise dialogue events and to form dialogue organisations to sustain the momentum of such work. He sought to build bridges between people of different religions, worldviews and backgrounds. Through his teachings and advice he sought to bridge the divide between science and religion, secular and religious worldviews,[2] leftists and rightists, Alevis and Sunnis and Turks and Kurds.[3] He used the arguments and idioms of religion and science to demonstrate the compatibility and indeed interdependence of the two, undermining the traditional dogmas on both sides which prevented people from meeting on common ground and developing a shared language.[4]

The kinds of dialogue efforts encouraged by Gülen are inclusive, open-ended and action-orientated, involve 'ordinary' people and lead to greater understanding. Gülen sees dialogue as a dynamic process which must be allowed to develop naturally,[5] including as wide a group of people as possible; thus it should be open-ended and inclusive.[6] For Gülen, dialogue itself consists not of dialogue events but

---

2   Louis J. Cantori, 'Fethullah Gülen: Kemalist and Islamic Republicanism and the Turkish Democratic Future,' in *Muslim World in Transition: Contributions of the Gülen Movement: Conference Proceedings*, ed. Ihsan Yilmaz et al. (London: Leeds Metropolitan University Press, 2007), 99.

3   Robert A Hunt and Yuksel A. Aslandogan. *Muslim Citizens of the Globalized World: Contributions of the Gülen Movement* (Somerset, N.J.: The Light, 2007), 57.

4   Fethullah Gülen, 'Science and Religion,' in *Knowledge and Responsibility: Islamic Perspectives on Science*, ed. Ali Ünal (Somerset, NJ: Tughra Books, 2007).

5   'Diyalog hizmetlerinde herşeyi baştan belirleyemezsiniz. Bazı şeyler vardır ki onları ancak ihtiyaçlar ve zaruretler belirler. Bu sistem statik değil sürekli hareket halinde olan ve kendini yenileyen dinamik bir sistemdir.' [trans: 'In dialogue, you cannot predetermine everything from the beginning. Some things can only be determined by needs and necessities. Therefore, dialogue is not a static system; it is in constant motion and is a self-renewing dynamic system.'] Fethullah Gülen, 'İkindi Sohbetleri' (Ahmet Kurucan lecture notes, Pennsylvania, 16th March, 2006).

6   Fethullah Gülen, *Criteria or Lights on the Way*, 2nd ed, (Izmir: Kaynak, 1998), vol. 1, 19.

of the interactions that occur as a result of such occasions. Those interactions must be allowed to develop and flourish, aided as appropriate by meetings, discussions and other projects. Dialogue initiatives should be 'action-orientated'[7] in the sense of moving beyond mere words and mutual well wishing to undertakings that bring about real, substantial, meaningful encounters.[8] Dialogue initiatives should engage the grass roots of society rather than only scholars or leaders.[9] [10] Finally, dialogue efforts should build mutual awareness and understanding.[11]

Gülen acknowledges that achieving grass root dialogue between ordinary people en masse will take a number of generations owing to entrenched prejudices. However, he states that the present generation must strive to do all it can to eradicate barriers and prejudices between people, helping to lay the foundations for real dialogue en masse in future generations.[12]

Gülen's understanding of dialogue is not based on pragmatism; it is not a strategy

---

7   Fethullah Gülen, *Toward a Global Civilization of Love & Tolerance* (Somerset, N.J.: Light, Inc, 2006), 50.

8   'Diyalog adına kuru söylemlere değil, harekete ihtiyaç var.' [trans: 'In dialogue, we do not need empty rhetoric; what we need is action.'] Fethullah Gülen, 'İkindi Sohbetleri' (Ahmet Kurucan lecture notes, Pennsylvania, 21st November, 2008).

9   Fethullah Gülen, *Toward a Global Civilizat n of Love & Tolerance*, 77; 'Diyalog'da önemli olan halkların halkla buluşmasıdır. Kalıcı ve başa.ılı olan diyalog ancak budur ve bu yolla gerçekleşir.' [trans: 'What is important in dialogue is for the grass roots/ordinary people ('halk') to meet with one another. Long-lasting and successful dialogue is only this and can only be achieved this way.'] Fethullah Gülen, 'İkindi Sohbetleri' (Ahmet Kurucan lecture notes, Pennsylvania, 23rd February, 2009). 'Çünkü esas olan taban kitlenin kendi arasında yaptığı diyalogdur. Kalıcı olan budur.' [trans: 'Because what matters is the dialogue that takes place between the grass roots of society. This is what will endure.'] Fethullah Gülen, 'İkindi Sohbetleri' (Ahmet Kurucan lecture notes, Pennsylvania, 6th April, 2009).

10   While Gülen states that dialogue should reach, include and rest upon the grass roots of society he is not claiming that everyone has an obligation to engage actively in dialogue.

11   Based on Gülen's inclusive understanding of dialogue, the Dialogue Society, a Gülen inspired organisation, defines dialogue as: 'meaningful interaction and exchange between people (often of different social, cultural, political, religious or professional groups) who come together through various kinds of conversations or activities with a view to increased understanding.' 'Our Approach,' Dialogue Society, accessed 25th March, 2013, http://www.dialoguesociety.org/about-us/our-approach.html.

12   'İnsanlığın geleceği adına bizim gelecek nesillere en büyük armağanımız geçmişten gelen kin ve nefreti toprağa gömmemiz ve kinsiz, nefretsiz bir dünyayı onlara teslim etmemizdir.' [trans: 'For the sake of humanity, our greatest gift to the future generations will be to bury the hatred and animosity of the past and pass on to them a world which is free of hatred and animosity.'] Fethullah Gülen, 'İkindi Sohbetleri' (Ahmet Kurucan lecture notes, Pennsylvania, 6th December, 2006).

to limit the threat posed by competing groups. Rather, it is deeply rooted in Islamic sources, such as the Qur'an, the Sunnah, *tasawwuf* (Sufism),[13] as well as nature, history, and contemporary perspectives. For Gülen, dialogue is a part of the fabric of Islam, embedded in its very foundation. It is a religious duty, not just encouraged but required by the values and commands of the Qur'an and Sunnah and by the basic character of our God-given human nature. Gülen advocates dialogue because of Islam, not despite it, and not on transient political grounds. Since Gülen's thought on dialogue is grounded in theology, it is possible to refer to his theory as a dialogue theology.[14]

Gülen considers dialogue to be inherently and instrumentally valuable. It is inherently valuable because it is in accordance with God's will and the character of His creation. We are social beings, intended to interact and learn about one another; the Qur'an states: 'We... made you into races and tribes so that you should get to know one another' (*al-Hujurat*, 49:13). Through knowing one another we come to know ourselves, which in turn helps us to know our Creator,[15] according to Gülen.[16] Since the diversity of creation manifests the diversity of God's names and attributes, knowledge of God's diverse creation contributes to our awareness of God.

Dialogue is instrumentally valuable for Gülen primarily because through dialogue people can cooperate and build durable solutions to shared problems. Dialogue is thus a means to community building and peace.

Gülen's approach is practice-focused, exemplified in the activities around the globe of the civil society movement he inspires. There is nothing abstract or esoteric about it. Gülen's history of constant interaction with the public and his profound sense of social responsibility keep his thought connected to practical matters and ordinary people. He is, nevertheless, a scholar, rooting his action in theology and making use of a distinctive range of concepts in his talks, articles and books. Let us

---

13   Sufism is the 'inner' dimension of Islam. Gülen defines it as the '[P]ath followed by an individual who, having been able to free himself or herself from human vices and weaknesses in order to acquire angelic qualities and conduct pleasing to God, lives in accordance with the requirements of God's knowledge and love, and in the resulting spiritual delight that ensues.' Fethullah Gülen, *Key Concepts in the Practice of Sufism Vol. 1* (Somerset, NJ: The Light, 2007), xii.

14   Writing from a perspective deeply influenced by Gülen's thinking, Ahmet Kurucan and Mustafa Kasim Erol provide a very useful idea of what Gülen's dialogue theology looks like in *Dialogue in Islam* (London: Dialogue Society, 2012).

15   Al-Ajluni, Kashf al-Khafa, 2:262.

16   Fethullah Gülen, *Key Concepts in the Practice of Sufism Vol. 1* (Somerset, NJ: The Light, 2007), 147.

now consider the underlying teachings and key concepts which are essential to the dialogue activities Gülen encourages.

A key point to note about Gülen's approach is that it is based on a human-centric discourse.[17] Because Gülen's worldview is God-centric his view on dialogue is human-centric.[18] Gülen believes that human beings are the greatest manifestation of God's names and attributes, that existence as we know it was created for the consciousness of human beings, that humans are God's vicegerents on earth,[19] that our humanity is our most basic commonality and that before God, in terms of being created all creation is equal.[20] This view of human beings brought about through a God-centric understanding of life and creation leads Gülen to believe that human beings should be respected and engaged with first and foremost because of their humanness. Their faith, religion and nationality come second and are irrelevant at this level of understanding. Showing respect to a fellow human being is a reflection of one's respect to God, his or her Creator. Gülen's vision of dialogue is centred on engagement at the level of our common humanity; his approach is thus inclusive and comprehensive.[21] One who truly embodies this approach becomes a 'gönül insanı' ('a person of the heart'), described by Gülen as follows:

> [they] open their hearts to everyone, welcoming them affectionately... Regarding their deeds and attributes, they try to be compatible with everybody, they try to avoid vicious competition with others,... they try to show as much respect as possible to the philosophy and ideas that other people adopt. They turn a blind eye to what other people may do wrong... [S]uch people nullify bad behaviour with kindness, not thinking to hurt anybody, even when they have been hurt over and over again.[22]

---

17   'Diyalog insanlarla insan olma ortak paydası etrafında toplanmaktır.' [trans: 'Dialogue is about humans coming together around their common humanity'.] Fethullah Gülen, 'İkindi Sohbetleri' (Ahmet Kurucan lecture notes, Pennsylvania, 14th January, 2006).

18   Fethullah Gülen, *Toward a Global Civilization of Love & Tolerance*, 50.

19   The role of vicegerent involves using God-given capacities to explore Creation, 'us[ing] everything to its purpose, and [being] the representatives of characteristics that belong to [God], such as knowledge, will, and might.' Fethullah Gülen, 'Humanity and its Responsibilities,' Fethullah Gülen website, last updated 14th June 2006, http://en.fgulen.com/love-and-tolerance/270-the-ideal-human/1829-humanity-and-its-responsibilities.

20   Fethullah Gülen, 'Longing for Love', *The Fountain*, 64 (2008).

21   Fethullah Gülen, *Toward a Global Civilization of Love and Tolerance*, 116-121.

22   Fethullah Gülen, 'Portrait of People of Heart,' Fethullah Gülen website, last updated 5th July 2007, http://fgulen .org/recent-articles/2234-the-portrait-of-people-of-heart.html.

An important element of Gülen's human-centric discourse is the belief that diversity is intended.[23] [24] Gülen considers that the Qur'an explicitly conceives of religion in the plural, referring to verses such as this: 'Had your Lord willed, all the people on earth would have believed. So can you [O Prophet] compel people to believe?' (*Yunus,* 10:99).[25] As already mentioned, the Qur'an connects human diversity to the divine intention that human beings should get to know one another (*al-Hujurat*, 49:13). For Gülen, diversity of race, religion, nation and life-way was intended by God and should be accepted and valued as a route to understanding. Diversity requires us to learn how to live together, which in turn necessitates dialogue. According to Gülen the response to diversity through positive engagement and dialogue is one of the major goals that the divine will has set for humankind.[26]

Gülen explains that the universe, in all its diversity, was created out of love and compassion.[27] As a result, love and compassion are an underlying theme of Gülen's discourse and shape his views on dialogue. He states that love and compassion should be the basis for all our interaction with one another.[28] They are the foundation of the active pursuit of peace and justice. Combined with spiritual awareness and a proper humility based on awareness of one's own impotence and insignificance, they make a person capable of real dialogue. But it is love and compassion which provide the necessary driving force for engagement in dialogue and other valuable social endeavours. Love's role of driving social action is crucial for Gülen, since in his eyes spirituality and spiritual practices fulfil their potential only when expressed through action in society.[29]

---

23   Gülen, *Toward a Global Civilization of Love and Tolerance,* 250.

24   'Herkesin Müslüman olmasını isteme farklı, Allah'ın iradesi farklı. Herkesin Müslüman olması hiçbir zaman olmamış, demek ki İlahi adet bu değil. Bunu görmemezlikten gelmemeli.' [trans: 'Wanting everyone to embrace Islam is one thing, what God wills is another thing. In the whole of history, never has the whole of mankind embraced Islam. This means that this is not God's tradition ('ilahi adet'). We should not overlook this point.'] Fethullah Gülen, 'İkindi Sohbetleri' (Ahmet Kurucan lecture notes, Pennsylvania, 14th June, 2009).

25   Other examples from the Qur'an included verses such as: 'Now the truth has come from your Lord: let those who wish to believe in it do so, and let those who wish to reject it do so,' (*al-Kahf,* 18:29) and 'There is no compulsion in religion' (*al-Baqarah,* 2:256).

26   Gülen, *Toward a Global Civilization of Love and Tolerance,* 249–50.

27   Gülen, *Toward a Global Civilization of Love and Tolerance,* 1, 4.

28   Gülen, *Toward a Global Civilization of Love and Tolerance,* 4.

29   Heon Kim and John Raines, *Making Peace, in and with the World: the Gülen Movement and Eco-Justice* (Newcastle upon Tyne: Cambridge Scholars, 2012), 59.

Gülen's counsel of love and compassion is complemented by his emphasis on humility and being non-judgemental towards others. This strong sense of humility[30] for Gülen is based on the following perspective: since everything is created and sustained through God, everything is dependent upon Him. As a result no one can take credit for any good that they do, as it is and can only be done in a state of dependence upon God. Therefore we must be humble in recognition of this fact whatever we achieve. We cannot judge others according to Gülen since we are all lost but for the mercy of God, and no one has the right to delimit the mercy of God but God Himself. Gülen advises, 'Be a prosecutor towards yourself, an advocate for others'.[31] This state of being is conducive to dialogue since it opens people up to one another and avoids the barriers to dialogue created by arrogant and judgemental attitudes.

Humility and being non-judgmental is also very important to achieve what Gülen calls *hoşgörü* (read *'hoshgoru'*), that is, empathic acceptance.[32] Gülen repeatedly states that dialogue is about empathic acceptance, that is accepting people as they are in their own right without judging or trying to change them, let alone convert them.[33] Empathic acceptance requires you to put yourself in the other's position. It puts the other at ease, allowing him to feel comfortable being himself around you, feeling that you appreciate him. Gülen says, 'there should be a chair for everyone within your heart.'[34]

Empathic acceptance is very useful in getting to know one another. When our engagement reaches a deeper level, though, how can we reconcile our own convictions with a readiness to support, learn from and borrow from the other? Regarding this point, Gülen expands on Said Nursi's engagement discourse.[35] He suggests that we should break the whole into its basic components such as actions and attributes and respond to these components individually, rather than judging the whole according to a particular part. In the case of another human being, we must love and respect him or her for the sake of his or her humanness. If we dislike something that a person does, we must limit our dislike to the attribute from which

---

30   Fethullah Gülen, 'Kriterler,' *Sızıntı* 226 (November, 1997).

31   Fethullah Gülen, 'Kriterler,' *Sızıntı* 226 (November, 1997).

32   David Capes, 'Tolerance in the Theology and Thought of A J Conyers and F Gülen,' in *Muslim World in Transition: Contributions of the Gülen Movement: Conference Proceedings,* ed. Ihsan Yilmaz et al (London: Leeds Metropolitan University Press, 2007), 429.

33   Fethullah Gülen, *Fasıldan Fasıla* 2 (İzmir: Nil Yayınları, 1996), 155-156.

34   Fethullah Gülen, 'Vicdan Genişliği ve Gerçek Şefkat,' Herkul website, 25th October, 2009, accessed 4th March, 2013, http://www.herkul.org/index.php/bamteli/bamteli-arsiv/7478-Vicdan.

35   Said Nursi, *Emirdağ Lahikâsı* (İstanbul: Söz Basım Yayın, 2004), 2, letter no. 151.

that action originates. For example, we should dislike the attribute of untruthfulness rather than the untruthful person.[36] The same principle applies when engaging with another culture or civilisation. We should not disregard a culture or civilisation due to certain qualities associated with it, but find ways of embracing the whole while maintaining reservations about those qualities. This approach provides a framework for dialogue at a deeper level in which participants engage openly without necessarily condoning one another's every attribute. It is a framework which may give dialogue participants confidence to engage wholeheartedly and borrow from one another without fear of having to compromise their own beliefs.[37]

Positive action (*müsbet hareket*)[38] is another important emphasis of Gülen's[39] which is very relevant to dialogue. The first point about positive action is that it implies and assumes action. Gülen has an acute sense of human responsibility towards God and towards all of His creation. For him, this responsibility requires conscious effort and action. 'Positive' action, for Gülen, is proactive, not formulated in reaction to someone else's action or position. Reacting to others, allowing them to determine your mode of action, is an uninspiring approach and indicative of a lack of belief in your own goals and methods. Positive action helps people to maintain a positive mind-set, whereas a reactive approach may incline them to perpetuate ongoing disputes and polemics. It involves a level-headedness, a calm, collected, consistent approach.

Positive action requires positive thinking about others (*hüsnüzan*) as opposed to seeing people in a negative light (*suizan*). Gülen points out that when we see others in this light, assuming the worst of them, we nurture a suspicious attitude towards

---

36   'Bizim inancımıza göre insan takdis edilecek varlıktır. Bizim tavrımız, temerrüde, tecavüze, zulme, bağye karşıdır. Yani vasıflaradır.' [trans: 'According to our belief, the human being is a blessed form of creation deserving of utmost respect. Our reaction is towards deception/ aggression, violence, oppression and tyranny. In other words, our reaction is towards attributes [of people, not people themselves.'] Fethullah Gülen, 'İkindi Sohbetleri' (Ahmet Kurucan lecture notes, Pennsylvania, 4th June, 2009).

37   'Evet; bir alış-veriş bu. Başka insanlar, gruplar, kültürler ve medeniyetlerde istifade edilecek değerler vardır; onları alıyoruz. Bizim de istifade edilecek değerlerimiz varsa, onları da veriyoruz.' [trans: 'Yes, this is a give and take. There are values we can benefit from in other people, groups, cultures and civilisations; these we take. If we have any values that are worth benefitting from, these we share.'] Fethullah Gülen, 'İkindi Sohbetleri' (Ahmet Kurucan lecture notes, Pennsylvania, 1st May, 2009).

38   Fethullah Gülen, 'Müsbet Hareketin Ölçüsü,' Fethullah Gülen Turkish website, 15th June, 2007, accessed 1st March, 2013, http://tr.fgulen.com/content/view/13920/3/.

39   'Müsbet Bütün Hizmetleri Alkışlayalım,' *Zaman*, 21st February, 2013, accessed 28th February, 2013, http://www.zaman.com.tr/gundem_musbet-butun-hizmetleri-alkislayalim_2056280.html.

them and a sense of superiority in ourselves.[40] *Suizan* destroys trust and goodwill and is incompatible with dialogue. *Hüsnüzan* as a key concept in *tasawwuf* and in Gülen's philosophy has two interconnected meanings; it can both signify thinking positively regarding God's designs and decrees,[41] and also thinking well of God's creatures, avoiding negative thoughts and feelings. In this sense, *hüsnüzan* in its comprehensive meaning refers to thinking positively and constructively about others, not taking other people's actions lightly, and avoiding focusing on other people's mistakes.[42] These positive attitudes are at the core of dialogue and proper social conduct in Gülen's thinking.

Having sketched some of the key concepts of Gülen's thinking on dialogue, it is worth noting his emphasis that the inclusivity, depth and range of true dialogue does not by any means imply homogenisation. Gülen is decidedly against dialogue being used to convert people or to create a melting pot in which people lose their distinct identities. He is also against people feeling the need to compromise their faith in order to achieve dialogue.[43] He often counsels people to be themselves in the process of dialogue. If people feel they have to conceal elements of their faith or religious practice or to engage in activities prohibited by their religion, Gülen states that this is no longer dialogue since it contravenes the essential principles of love, compassion, humility and empathic acceptance.

---

40   Fethullah Gülen, 'Measure of Selflessness,' Fethullah Gülen website, 16th April 2010, accessed 26th December 2012, http://fgulen.org/recent-articles/3608-measure-of-selflessness.html.

41   John Renard, *A to Z of Sufism* (Plymouth: Scarecrow Press, 2005), 265.

42   Fethullah Gülen 'Başkalarına hüsnüzan nazarıyla bakmak,' Fethullah Gülen Turkish website, 19th December, 2011, accessed 26th December, 2012, http://tr.fgulen.com/content/view/20027/3/.

43   Ahmet Kurucan and Mustafa K. Erol, *Dialogue in Islam* (London: Dialogue Society, 2012), 20-22.

Theory and Practice

Through his teachings and sermons, Fethullah Gülen has inspired a transnational civil society movement engaging in education and dialogue, contributing towards more positive relations between groups of different faiths, cultures and political positions. The movement is faith inspired yet faith neutral in its activities and is increasingly attracting support from people of diverse backgrounds and religions. The movement is loosely connected through shared ideals and teachings, some of which were explored above. In this section, we will consider how Gülen's teachings on dialogue are being put into practice.

Many people involved in or familiar with the movement inspired by Gülen consider that his teachings and advocacy have attuned a large mass of people to a dialogical outlook in their general approach to interpersonal and inter-group relations. This is attributed mainly to two reasons. First, Gülen's general exposition of Islam has always been very inclusive, loving and peaceful, inherently dialogic. Ordinary people influenced by his scholarship have thus adopted a dialogic outlook in their faith. The second reason is that Gülen expressly argues that dialogue is too important to be left to dialogue practitioners or dialogue organisations alone.[44] These people and organisations may have a particular specialism and expertise in dialogue but their efforts must be supported through the collective will of wider society and organisations not explicitly focused on dialogue. To achieve this, all people should be dialogically predisposed, that is respectful of diversity, welcoming and ready to engage, and all organisations, whatever their primary purpose, should utilise dialogue in the course of pursuing their main objectives. In accordance with this view, those people and organisations inspired by Gülen, whether schools, universities, clinics, relief charities, business associations or others, share a commitment to a dialogic approach and to bringing about a more humane, loving, caring and peaceful society.

Schools guided by the principles of Gülen's vision have been founded in around 150 countries. In regions affected by ongoing or recent conflict, including Afghanistan, Pakistan, the Philippines, Bosnia-Herzegovina, southeast Turkey and northern Iraq, the schools, which welcome students from diverse backgrounds, play an important role in easing inter-group tensions.[45] This role is noted by Father Thomas Michel SJ with reference to examples such as the Philippine-Turkish School of Tolerance on the southern Philippine Island of Mindanao. He visited the school in 1995, at a

---

44   Gülen, *Toward a Global Civilization of Love and Tolerance*, 77.

45   Harun Akyol, 'How to Solve the Kirkuk Problem?' *Today's Zaman*, 20th April, 2011, accessed 5th March, 2013,   http://todayszaman.com/news-241508-how-to-solve-the-kirkuk-problem-by-harun-akyol*.html.

time when the area was ravaged by all kinds of inter-community violence. Around half the school's students were Muslim and half Christian. Michel states that the school offered them, 'an excellent education and a more positive way of living and relating to each other.'[46]

From the large pool of people and organisations inspired by Gülen, organisations focused specifically on dialogue have emerged alongside educational initiatives. Because the movement is not centrally organised it is not possible to determine the number of Gülen inspired dialogue organisations, but it is safe to assume that there are Gülen inspired dialogue organisations in approximately 150 countries.[47] Gülen is not officially linked to any of them, accept a handful of which he is the honorary chairman, such as the Journalists and Writers Foundation in Istanbul[48], the Rumi Forum[49] in Washington DC and the Intercultural Dialogue Platform[50] in Brussels.

Like these, the Dialogue Society is a Gülen inspired organisation. The Dialogue Society's guiding principles, summarised below, have been inferred from Gülen's teachings and key concepts, which we explored in the previous section. Other Gülen inspired organisations may have arrived at the same or similar approaches given the shared source of inspiration and guidance. Naturally, the list is not exhaustive.

1. To formulate dialogue in the most inclusive way possible

2. While founded and led by Muslims, to be an organisation serving mainstream society

3. To allow dialogue to be dynamic, being open to new developments, forms of engagement and projects

4. To balance dynamism and development with consistency and perseverance

5. To come together around humanness

6. To embrace everyone with love, compassion and empathic acceptance

---

46 Thomas Michel, 'Fethullah Gülen as Educator,' in *Turkish Islam and the Secular State: The Gülen Movement,* ed. M Hakan Yavuz and John L. Esposito (Syra Cruz: Syra Cruz University Press, 2003), 70.

47 One of various indicators suggesting this approximate figure is the presence of Gülen inspired schools in this number of countries; in general, since dialogue organisations can be more easily established than schools, it is likely that those inspired by Gülen will have set up a dialogue organisation in a country where they are also able to found a school.

48 This is the first Gülen inspired dialogue organisation, founded in 1994. Journalists and Writers Foundation, accessed 7th March, 2013, http://www.gyv.org.tr/.

49 Rumi Forum, accessed 5th March, 2013, http://www.rumiforum.org/about/about-rumi-forum.html.

50 Intercultural Dialogue Platform, accessed 5th March, 2013, http://www.dialogueplatform.eu/.

7. To insist on peace as the default position

8. To recognise that dialogue is inherently as well as instrumentally valuable

9. To be mindful that dialogue is a natural human expression and that diversity is an intended phenomenon

10. To ensure that dialogue and its activities are positive and proactive and focused on developing greater understanding and trust

11. To focus on core social issues, developing a stronger sense of belonging and concern for one another

12. To be locally driven and motivated, working towards facilitating dialogue within the society in which the organisation is based.

Based on such guiding principles, Gülen inspired dialogue charities worldwide undertake tens of thousands of dialogue initiatives and projects each year, trying to reach out to the disengaged. These charities organise events at various levels, targeting the grass roots of society as well as academics, journalists, policy-makers and community leaders. The Dialogue Society aims to advance social cohesion by connecting communities, empowering people to engage and contributing to the development of ideas on dialogue and community building. It brings people together through discussion forums, courses, capacity building publications and outreach. It operates nation-wide with regional branches across the UK. Through a Master's Degree in Dialogue Studies,[51] the launch of a Journal of Dialogue Studies,[52] a Dialogue School[53] and this very book on dialogue theories it aims amongst other things to contribute towards establishing 'dialogue' as a distinct academic field. It is hoped that the development of such a field will build further momentum for the development of dialogic approaches and initiatives.

---

51   The MA in Dialogue Studies was developed and is delivered in partnership with Keele University. 'Dialogue Studies MA,' Dialogue Society, accessed 5th March, 2013, http://www.dialoguesociety.org/courses/dialogue-studies-ma.html.

52   'Journal of Dialogue Studies,' Dialogue Society, accessed 5th March, 2013, http://www.dialoguesociety.org/publications/academia/829-journal-of-dialogue-studies.html.

53   'Dialogue School', Dialogue Society, accessed 5th March, 2013, http://www.dialoguesociety.org/courses/dialogue-school.html.

Questions for Reflection

1. Gülen's teachings have had an immense impact, not only in Turkey but also internationally. What makes him so influential?

2. Are there any limits to the practice of *hüsnüzan*, in the sense of thinking the best of others? Can *hüsnüzan* be practised sincerely and consistently without naivety?

3. How does one become a 'person of the heart' (*gönül insanı*)?

4. Gülen's description of dialogue includes different types of activities and conversations that bring people together and result in greater understanding. He states that lasting dialogue will only be achieved if it includes and rests on the grass roots of society. How can dialogue (as defined by Gülen) be extended to include grass roots of society?

5. Are there any limits to 'positive action' and 'empathic acceptance' (*müsbet hareket* and *hoşgörü*)? If so, what are they?

6. While volunteers of the Hizmet movement seek to promote an inclusive dialogue between diverse groups, the majority of them are inspired by and rooted in the same Islamic faith. What advantages and disadvantages might be associated with this fact?

Bibliography

Akyol, Harun. 'How to Solve the Kirkuk Problem?' *Today's Zaman*, 20 April, 2011. Accessed 5th March, 2013. http://todayszaman.com/news-241508-how-to-solve-the-kirkuk-problem-by-harun-akyol*.html.

Cantori, Louis J. 'Fethullah Gülen: Kemalist and Islamic Republicanism and the Turkish Democratic Future.' In *Muslim World in Transition: Contributions of the Gülen Movement: Conference Proceedings,* edited by Ihsan Yilmaz et al., 77-103. London: Leeds Metropolitan University Press, 2007.

Capes, David. 'Tolerance in the Theology and Thought of A J Conyers and F Gülen.' In *Muslim World in Transition: Contributions of the Gülen Movement: Conference Proceedings*, edited by Ihsan Yilmaz et al., 428-429. London: Leeds Metropolitan University Press, 2007.

Dialogue Society. Accessed 25th March, 2013. www.dialoguesociety.org.

Fethullah Gülen Turkish website. 'Başkalarına hüsnüzan nazarıyla bakmak.' Accessed 26th December, 2012. http://tr.fgulen.com/content/view/20027/3/

Gülen, Fethullah. *Criteria or Lights on the Way*, 2nd ed. Izmir: Kaynak, 1998.

Gülen, Fethullah. *Fasıldan Fasıla* 2. Izmir: Nil Yayınları, 1996.

Gülen, Fethullah. 'Humanity and its Responsibilities.' Fethullah Gülen website. Last updated 14th June 2006. http://en.fgulen.com/love-and-tolerance/270-the-ideal-human/1829-humanity-and-its-responsibilities.

Gülen, Fethullah. *Key Concepts in the Practice of Sufism Vol. 1*. Somerset, NJ: The Light, 2007.

Gülen, Fethullah. 'Kriterler.' *Sızıntı* 226 (November 1997).

Gülen, Fethullah. 'Measure of Selflessness.' Fethullah Gülen website, 16th April 2010. Accessed 26th December, 2012. http://www.fethullahgulen.org/gulens-works/296-recent-articles/3608-measure-of-selflessness.html.

Gülen, Fethullah. 'Müsbet Hareketin Ölçüsü.' Fethullah Gülen Turkish website, 15th June, 2007. Accessed 1st March, 2013. http://tr.fgulen.com/content/view/13920/3/.

Gülen, Fethullah. 'Portrait of People of Heart.' Fethullah Gülen website. Last updated 5th July 2007. http://fgulen.org/recent-articles/2234-the-portrait-of-people-of-heart.html.

Gülen, Fethullah. 'Science and Religion.' In *Knowledge and Responsibility: Islamic Perspectives on Science*, edited by Ali Ünal. Somerset, NJ: Tughra Books, 2007.

Gülen, Fethullah. *Toward a Global Civilization of Love & Tolerance*. Somerset, NJ: Light, Inc, 2006.

Gülen, Fethullah. 'Vicdan Genişliği ve Gerçek Şefkat.' Herkul website, 25th October, 2009. Accessed 4th March, 2013. http://www.herkul.org/index.php/bamteli/bamteli-arsiv/7478-Vicdan.

Hunt, Robert A. and Yuksel A. Aslandogan. *Muslim Citizens of the Globalized World: Contributions of the Gülen Movement*. Somerset, NJ: The Light, 2007.

Intercultural Dialogue Platform. Accessed 5th March, 2013. http://www. dialogueplatform.eu/.

Journalists and Writers Foundation. Accessed 7th March, 2013. http://www.gyv. org.tr/.

Kim, Heon and John Raines. *Making Peace, in and with the World: the Gülen Movement and Eco-Justice.* New Castle upon Tyne: Cambridge Scholars, 2011.

Kurucan, Ahmet and Mustafa Kasim Erol. *Dialogue in Islam.* London: Dialogue Society, 2012.

Michel, Thomas. 'Fethullah Gülen as Educator.' In *Turkish Islam and the Secular State: The Gülen Movement,* edited by M Hakan Yavuz and John L. Esposito, 67-82. Syra Cruz: Syra Cruz University Press, 2003.

Nursi, Said. *Emirdağ Lahikâsı.* Istanbul: Söz Basım Yayın, 2004.

Renard, John. *A to Z of Sufism.* Plymouth: Scarecrow Press, 2005.

Rumi Forum. Accessed 5th March, 2013. http://www.rumiforum.org/about/about-rumi-forum.html.

Ünal, Ali ed. *Knowledge and Responsibility: Islamic Perspectives on Science.* Somerset, NJ: Tughra Books, 2007.

Yilmaz, Ihsan, Eileen Barker, Henri J. Barkey, Muhammad Abdul Haleem, George S. Harris, Thomas Michel, Simon Robinson, Zeki Saritoprak, David Thomas, Paul Weller, Ian G. Williams, Alan Godlas, Asaf Hussain, Johnston McMaster, Colin Turner and Tim Winter, eds. *Muslim World in Transition: Contributions of the Gülen Movement: Conference Proceedings.* London: Leeds Metropolitan University Press, 2007.

Zaman. 'Müsbet Bütün Hizmetleri Alkışlayalım.' *Zaman,* 21st February, 2013. Accessed 28th February, 2013. http://www.zaman.com.tr/gundem_musbet-butun-hizmetleri-alkislayalim_2056280.html.

Recommended Reading

Gülen's Works:

Gülen, Fethullah. *Key Concepts in the Practice of Sufism Vol. 1.* Somerset, NJ: The Light, Inc., 2007.

Gülen, Fethullah. *Key Concepts in the Practice of Sufism Vol 2.* Somerset, NJ: The Light, Inc., 2004.

Gülen, Fethullah. *Key Concepts in the Practice of Sufism Vol. 3.* Clifton, NJ: Tughra Books, 2009.

Gülen, Fethullah. *Key Concepts in the Practice of Sufism Vol. 4.* Clifton, NJ: Tughra Books, 2010.

Gülen, Fethullah. *Speech and Power of Expression.* Clifton, NJ: Tughra Books, 2010.

Gülen, Fethullah. *Toward a Global Civilization of Love & Tolerance.* Somerset, NJ: Light, Inc, 2006.

Commentary:

Barton, Greg, Paul Weller and Ihsan Yilmaz eds. *The Muslim World and Politics in Transition: Creative Contributions of the Gülen Movement.* London, New Delhi, New York and Sydney: Bloomsbury, 2013.

Carroll, Jill B. *A Dialogue of Civilisations: Gülen's Islamic Ideals and Humanistic Discourse.* Somerset, NJ: The Light, 2007.

Ergil, Doğu. *Fethullah Gülen & the Gülen Movement in 100 Questions.* New York, NY: Blue Dome PR, 2012.

Ünal, Ali and Alphonse Williams. *Advocate of Dialogue: Fethullah Gülen.* Fairfax, Virginia: The Fountain, 2000.

Weller, Paul, and Ihsan Yilmaz. *European Muslims, Civility and Public Life: Perspectives on and from the Gülen Movement.* London: Continuum, 2012.

Practical Applications:

Çelik, Gürkan. *The Gülen Movement: Building Social Cohesion through Dialogue and Education.* Nieuwegein: Eburon, 2010.

Dialogue Society. Accessed 25th March, 2013. http://www.dialoguesociety.org.

Esposito, John L. and Ihsan Yilmaz eds. *Islam and Peacebuilding: Gülen Movement Initiatives*. Blue Dome Press, 2010.

Fethullah Gülen website (English). Accessed 28th March, 2013. http://www.en.fgulen.com/.

Hunt, Robert A., and Yüksel A. Aslandogan. *Muslim Citizens of the Globalized World: Contributions of the Gülen Movement*. Somerset, NJ: The Light, 2007.

Journalists and Writers Foundation. Accessed 7th March, 2013. http://www.gyv.org.tr/.

Kalyoncu, Mehmet. *A Civilian Response to Ethno-Religious Conflict*. Somerset, NJ: The Light, 2008.

Kim, Heon and John Raines. *Making Peace, in and with the World: the Gülen Movement and Eco-Justice*. New Castle upon Tyne: Cambridge Scholars, 2011.

Kurucan, Ahmet and Mustafa Kasim Erol. *Dialogue in Islam*. London: Dialogue Society, 2012.

Tenzin Gyatso, the Fourteenth Dalai Lama

Biographical Introduction

The Fourteenth Dalai Lama, the religious leader of the Gelug sect of Tibetan Buddhism, is undoubtedly one of the contemporary world's most loved and revered spiritual leaders. Despite the many trials he has faced in his lifetime, he is known for his unfailing warmth and infectious laugh; he calls himself a 'professional laugher'.[1] He has, by all accounts, a gift for dialogue, which is surely related to his propensity to relate to everyone he meets as to an old friend, with directness and tangible goodwill. American professor of religious studies Thomas Forsthoefel describes his meeting with the Dalai Lama: 'the Dalai Lama took both my hands and gazed at me... I became aware that [he] was doing something that far transcended typical mundane encounters... [it] was something deeper and more penetrating.'[2] We might say that the Dalai Lama is a master of that direct person-to-person encounter that Martin Buber calls 'dialogue'.[3]

He was born in 1935, to a peasant family in a small village in north-eastern Tibet. His mother, he recalls, was a valuable early influence, a woman of great compassion.[4] When he was two, the religious authorities determined that he was the reincarnation of the recently deceased thirteenth Dalai Lama, and hence Tibet's future spiritual and political leader. He was taken to the capital, Lhasa, ready to begin the extensive education required to prepare him for that role.

At sixteen he was forced prematurely to take on political power when Tibet was invaded by the Chinese. They gradually extended their control over the country until, in 1959, the Dalai Lama had to escape to India. Since that time he has continually sought to engage the Chinese authorities in dialogue and has rallied international support for his oppressed people. He has consistently exhorted Tibetans not to resort to violence, however great their suffering and frustration. On receiving the Nobel Peace Prize in 1989 he said that the honour was a tribute to his 'mentor' Mahatma Gandhi, whose commitment to nonviolence greatly inspired

---

1   Tenzin Gyatso, the Fourteenth Dalai Lama, *My Spiritual Autobiography* (London: Rider, 2010), 23.

2   Thomas A. Forsthoefel ed., *The Dalai Lama: Essential Writings* (Maryknoll, New York: Orbis Books, 2008), 13 f.

3   See our chapter on Martin Buber in the present volume.

4   Tenzin Gyatso, *My Spiritual Autobiography,* 11.

him.[5] In exile he led the development of a democratic government for Tibet. He fully retired from his political role in 2011, while retaining his role of spiritual leadership.

The Dalai Lama is a well-known advocate and practitioner of interfaith dialogue. He has engaged in dialogue with religious leaders of diverse faiths, including three popes, and has spoken against distorted portrayals of Islam following the terrorist attacks of 2001.[6] He has been a key part of the development of dialogue between Buddhist and Christian monks and nuns. He has also facilitated a long series of dialogues between Buddhist practitioners and scientists.[7]

The Dalai Lama may be an exceptional person, but he has a very practical outlook and we can learn concrete lessons from his approach. In his practice of dialogue in a range of contexts we can identify guiding principles which deserve our consideration.

---

5   See Alan Jacobs, ed., *Masters of Wisdom: His Holiness the Dalai Lama: Infinite Compassion for an Imperfect World* (London: Watkins Publishing, 2011), 148. Gandhi himself never received the Nobel Peace Prize.

6   Robert Thurman, *Why the Dalai Lama Matters* (Atria Books/Beyond Words Publishing, 2008), 52.

7   See Swati Chopra, 'Gentle Bridges and Golden Seeds: the Dalai Lama's Dialogues with Science,' in *Understanding the Dalai Lama*, ed. Rajiv Mehtotra (London: Penguin Books, 2006), 146-158.

Thought on Dialogue

In this section we will explore the principles which can be inferred from the Dalai Lama's approaches to dialogue for conflict resolution and interfaith dialogue, and briefly note his approach to dialogue between science and religious practitioners. First, though, let us consider the key values and characteristics underlying his practice and statements in all these areas.

Like Fethullah Gülen, also introduced in this volume, the Dalai Lama has an acute sense of our shared humanity. 'Ultimately,' he writes, 'each of us is just a human being, like everyone else: we all desire happiness and do not want suffering.' Further, we are utterly interdependent. We cannot survive without others, as we quickly see when we reflect on our needs when very young, very old or unwell. Because we are social beings who need others, compassion towards others is ultimately in all our interests.[8]

It is also in our nature, as seen in the powerful and immediate bond of affection between a mother and her newborn child. Compassion, *nying-je* in Tibetan, is central to the Dalai Lama's conception of ethics. Based on empathy, 'the ability to enter into and, to some extent, share others' suffering,' it can be developed to different degrees, through practice and meditation.[9] Fully developed compassion is universal, extending to all sentient beings. One meditation used by the Dalai Lama focuses on the Buddhist idea that, since all creatures have been through countless reincarnations, at some point in the past, each of them has been our mother and nurtured us; this reflection encourages great compassion towards all sentient beings.[10]

Compassion, and a sense of shared humanity, are both reflected in the Dalai Lama's widely appreciated warm and personal manner. He states, 'I try to treat whoever I meet as an old friend.'[11]

A final element of his approach worth noting here is his intellectual curiosity. Thomas Forstoefel notes his early friendship with German mountaineer Heinrich Harrer, whom he questioned constantly about the West. Forstoefel notes, 'This congenital curiosity has carried over into adulthood, as he has convened or participated in numerous conferences and opportunities to bring together scholars, thinkers and religious leaders.'[12]

---

8   Jacobs, ed., *Masters of Wisdom: His Holiness the Dalai Lama*, 31, 40.

9   Tenzin Gyatso, the Fourteenth Dalai Lama, *Ancient Wisdom, Modern World: Ethics for the New Millennium* (London: Little, Brown and Company, 1999), 131.

10   Forsthoefel ed., *The Dalai Lama: Essential Writings*, 123 ff.

11   'Compassion and the Individual,' Office of His Holiness the 14th Dalai Lama, accessed 27th July, 2012, http://www.dalailama.com/messages/compassion/.

12   Forsthoefel ed., *The Dalai Lama: Essential Writings*, 130.

We can now turn our attention to the Dalai Lama's approach to dialogue, firstly, in the context of international conflict resolution. He sees dialogue as indispensable in this context. In a speech at the European Parliament in Strasbourg, 2001, he stated, 'Dialogue is the only sensible and intelligent way of resolving differences and clashes of interests, whether between individuals or nations.'[13]

This statement reflects one of the key principles of his approach to dialogue for conflict resolution: absolute commitment to nonviolence. This commitment does not depend on a reciprocal commitment by other parties. The Dalai Lama has been creative in using international political and media pressure to try to persuade the Chinese authorities to negotiate over Tibet, but resorting to violence has always been out of the question, regardless of the violence and oppression inflicted on Tibetans. In 2008 he threatened to relinquish his political leadership if his people turned to violence.[14] As well as being a matter of principle, the Dalai Lama sees nonviolence as the only path to a sustainably peaceful solution.[15] Robert Thurman notes the great potential of this approach, suggesting that 'many conflicts around the world could certainly be solved if the option of a resort to violence were taken off the table,' opening the way to calm and constructive discussion by reducing levels of fear and thus of anger.[16]

For the Dalai Lama, non-violence, *ahimsa* in Buddhist terms, requires one to refrain from harming others specifically on the basis of compassion. Refraining from harming others out of fear or indifference is not non-violence. Non-violence and compassion are two sides of the same coin.[17] The Dalai Lama's absolute commitment to nonviolence is grounded in his commitment to universal compassion, which demands an attitude of kindness and concern even towards 'enemies' or oppressors. While speaking of the plight of Tibetans in his 1989 Nobel Peace Prize Lecture, he stated:

> I speak not with a feeling of anger or hatred towards those who are responsible for the immense suffering of our people and the destruction of our land, homes and culture. They too are human beings who struggle to find happiness and deserve our compassion.[18]

---

13   Thurman, *Why the Dalai Lama Matters,* 111.

14   Forsthoefel ed., *The Dalai Lama: Essential Writings,* 131.

15   Senthil Ram, 'The Dalai Lama as a Political Strategist,' in *Understanding the Dalai Lama,* 168 f.

16   Thurman, *Why the Dalai Lama Matters,* 86.

17   'Non Violence and Ethical Values,' Office of His Holiness the 14th Dalai Lama, accessed 15th January, 2013, http://www.dalailama.com/webcasts/post/252-non-violence-and-ethical-values.

18   Jacobs, ed., *Masters of Wisdom: His Holiness the Dalai Lama,* 143.

People who have met the Dalai Lama testify to the sincerity of this impressive attitude. He himself has spoken with humble admiration of the 'wonderful' example of another Tibetan Buddhist monk who, after over twenty years of imprisonment and torture, stated that his worst fear had been that he might lose his compassion for his tormentors.[19]

The combination of the Dalai Lama's genuine compassion for all parties and his pragmatic concern to find solutions that will last ground two further principles of dialogue for conflict resolution: concern to find mutually beneficial solutions to conflict, and readiness to make concessions. His 1988 'Five Point Peace Plan' for Tibet and China made a major concession to Chinese interests by not insisting on Tibetan independence. He proposed autonomy for Tibet in the context of voluntary union with China. The Dalai Lama considers that this solution would be mutually beneficial and thus sustainable:

> [it] would greatly enhance the international image of China and contribute to her stability and unity – the two topmost priorities of Beijing – while at the same time the Tibetans would be ensured of the basic rights and freedoms to preserve their own civilization and to protect the delicate environment of the Tibetan Plateau.[20]

The Dalai Lama is aware that solutions to conflict depend on the development of trust. As Thurman notes, for his Five Point Peace Plan to be successful, 'China would need to trust his pledge to lead his people in voting for union, and to trust the Tibetans' love and trust of him.' 'This,' Thurman explains, 'is why he has been so keen to travel to China and meet its leaders privately, to convince them of his sincerity.'[21] He believes firmly in the importance of building trust and positive relationships through personal meetings. His support for various international summit meetings, in which world leaders meet one another personally, comes from this same conviction.[22]

Ultimately, the building of mutual understanding and trust through personal encounters must happen at two levels for conflict resolution to be successful and sustainable. Sincere dialogue is needed both between leaders and at the grass roots. In the case of Tibet and China this means dialogue between the Tibetan Government in Exile and the government of the People's Republic of China, and

---

19   Mary Craig, 'A Very Human Human Being,' in *Understanding the Dalai Lama*, 75.

20   2001 Strasbourg speech. See Thurman, *Why the Dalai Lama Matters*, 115.

21   Thurman, *Why the Dalai Lama Matters*, 70.

22   Thurman, *Why the Dalai Lama Matters*, 66.

between ordinary Tibetan and Chinese people.[23]

A final principle embodied in the Dalai Lama's approach to the situation with China is persistence. He steadfastly refuses to give up on dialogue. At Strasbourg in 2001, although, after long decades of efforts, China was still continuing to refuse to enter into serious negotiations, he reaffirmed his belief in and commitment to dialogue.[24]

Let us now move on to consider the Dalai Lama's approach to interfaith dialogue. For the Dalai Lama, dialogue is the key to interreligious harmony. Interreligious harmony depends on 'appreciation of the others' faith traditions', an understanding of what their traditions mean to them and the moral guidance they find in them.[25] Dialogue is the best way to achieve such understanding. It also allows followers of different religions to learn from the practices and moral insights of others.[26]

The Dalai Lama has advocated four particular forms of dialogue between people of different faith traditions. These are:

1. 'Discussions among scholars in which the convergence and perhaps more importantly the divergence between faith traditions are explored and appreciated...'

2. 'Encounters between ordinary but practicing followers of different religions in which each shares their experiences. This is perhaps the most effective way of appreciating others' teachings.'

3. '...occasional meetings between religious leaders joining together to pray for a common cause.'

4. '...members of different faith traditions going on joint pilgrimages together.'[27]

The Dalai Lama's own practice of these various forms of dialogue might be characterised as personal, positive and profound. From it, and from his statements about interfaith dialogue, we can extract a number of key principles.

The first principle to note is respect for difference and the rejection of proselytism. When giving a talk on Buddhism to a non-Buddhist audience, he actively asks

---

23   Ram, 'The Dalai Lama as a Political Strategist,' in *Understanding the Dalai Lama*, 167.

24   Thurman, *Why the Dalai Lama Matters*, 118.

25   Tenzin Gyatso, *Ancient Wisdom, Modern World: Ethics for the New Millennium*, 122.

26   Forsthoefel ed., *The Dalai Lama: Essential Writings*, 139, 141.

27   Tenzin Gyatso, *Ancient Wisdom, Modern World: Ethics for the New Millennium*, 122 f.

them not to take what he says as a call to adopt Buddhism.[28] From his perspective, religions teach the same core moral values in different ways, each being uniquely suited to the needs of its own followers.[29] He sees great value in all religions, and urges others to explore different religions through dialogue, gain appreciation for them and learn from their distinctive practices and moral insights. Respect for all religions and 'total faith' in one's own are, he holds, entirely compatible.[30]

He has an inclusive outlook. Thurman notes that 'one of [his] innovations in interreligious dialogue has been to issue a call to secularists to join the dialogue, since their world-view is itself a sort of religion, in the sense of a belief system.' Dialogue can help people of all kinds of belief systems to reach greater mutual understanding and to identify and affirm vital common moral values such as compassion.[31]

He advocates the open exploration of sensitive issues in interfaith dialogue. Speaking of problems between the majority and the minority he emphasises that 'both sides should not take lightly the sensitive issues between themselves.' Harmony requires proper mutual understanding, and that requires 'dialogue, dialogue and dialogue!' 'Both sides,' he states, 'should discuss and clearly express what they think about the other's view and opinion.'[32]

This kind of open exploration of issues works best where there is also openness to presence and readiness for friendship. Father Laurence Freeman describes how the Dalai Lama's embodiment of these qualities paved the way for a profound dialogue at the groundbreaking John Main seminar of 1994, when, the first non-Christian to lead the seminar, he was invited to explore the Christian Gospels with Catholic monks and nuns. Freeman explains how his example of openness and warmth led others to engage in the same spirit, providing a foundation of mutual openness that made successful verbal dialogue possible.[33]

For the Dalai Lama, proper dialogue in any context is essentially personal. As

---

28   Thurman, *Why the Dalai Lama Matters*, 48 f. Conscious of the profound psychological and social impact of changing one's religion he suggests that in most cases it is more helpful for someone to learn from other religions and bring certain lessons from them into one's own practice than to convert to a different religion.

29   Forsthoefel ed., *The Dalai Lama: Essential Writings*, 134 f.

30   Jacobs, ed., *Masters of Wisdom: His Holiness the Dalai Lama*, 99.

31   Thurman, *Why the Dalai Lama Matters*, 52.

32   Jacobs, ed., *Masters of Wisdom: His Holiness the Dalai Lama*, 100.

33   Laurence Freeman OSB, introduction to *The Good Heart: a Buddhist Perspective on the Teachings of Jesus*, by Tenzin Gyatso, the Fourteenth Dalai Lama (Somerville, MA: Wisdom Publications, 1996), 5 ff.

we have seen, he considers that people understand the meaning and value of one another's traditions best when they speak to one another from their own personal experience. He states that his appreciation of the meaning of Christianity, and its moral and spiritual worth for its followers, came from heart-to-heart conversations with the Cistercian monk Thomas Merton.[34]

Another feature of the Dalai Lama's approach is the serious seeking of in-depth understanding of the other's faith, in all its difference and uniqueness. This comes through in the detailed report on the content of the 1994 John Main seminar in the Dalai Lama's book *The Good Heart*. Taking the Dalai Lama's comments on the Gospels as their starting point, participants went on to carefully explore religious ideas from rebirth to the place of rationality in religion. The Dalai Lama and his dialogue partners asked one another many questions to reach fuller understanding, respectfully noting marked differences as well as common ground between the faiths.[35] As Freeman notes, the Dalai Lama 'believes in respecting, and indeed reverencing, the unique characteristics of each religion,' and approaches opportunities to learn about them with great eagerness.[36]

In his various dialogues with Christian monks and nuns, which feature periods of silent meditation, we see that, for the Dalai Lama, silence in dialogue is as important as speech. Freeman explains that while the intellectual explorations of the John Main seminar were highly valuable, bringing fuller mutual and self-understanding, participants enjoyed 'a deeper experience' during periods of silence. In silence, he writes, 'uniqueness and difference, along with other dualities, coincide: they meet in a unity that respects and fulfils difference and at the same time transcends division. This is love.'[37]

Clearly, for the Dalai Lama, dialogue is not limited to conversation. Indeed, as we saw above, he considers that dialogue can take the form of a range of shared activities, including joint prayer for peace and interfaith pilgrimages, in which people gain appreciation of each other's traditions by physically stepping into one

---

34   Tenzin Gyatso, *Ancient Wisdom, Modern World: Ethics for the New Millennium*, 123.

35   The Dalai Lama recounts how, on another occasion, the Christian Benedictine monk Bede Griffiths answered a question that had long perplexed him, explaining why it is that Christians reject the notion of rebirth. The Dalai Lama reports that he 'found the explanation deeply convincing.' Without sharing Griffiths' perspective he could acutely appreciate the Christian rationale that he explained, clearly valuing the insight provided on the distinctive theological and moral world of Christianity. See Tenzin Gyatso, *The Good Heart*, 58 f.

36   Freeman, introduction to *The Good Heart*, 16.

37   Freeman, introduction to *The Good Heart*, 19.

another's religious worlds. Such shared experiences and actions can strengthen mutual understanding and regard and unite different communities around common values and concerns.

In the Dalai Lama's dialogues with science, we see many of the same characteristics and principles at work as in his practice of interfaith dialogue. We noted in our chapter on the physicist David Bohm that the Dalai Lama engaged in dialogue with him on a number of occasions. The two thinkers engaged in a shared enquiry into the interconnectedness of all life, drawing on insights both from Buddhism and from physics. The Dalai Lama has a serious, ongoing interest in engagement with scientific perspectives. Since 1987 he has been engaging with scientists from different fields at a series of 'Mind and Life' dialogues.[38] In such dialogue, as in interfaith dialogue, he sees clear potential for important mutual learning. Buddhism's deep exploration of the mind can, through dialogue, contribute to further scientific understanding. Dialogue with Buddhism can also help science to stay in touch with fundamental human values. At the same time, modern science can offer interesting objective analysis of Buddhism's techniques and potentially help to make elements of them more readily available to a wider public.[39]

We will take a further look at the 'Mind and Life' dialogues in the 'Theory and Practice' section. Let us note here, though, that these dialogues are again characterised by an eager seeking of in-depth understanding of the other's perspective, a respectful acknowledgement of real difference and an atmosphere of openness and friendship fostered by the Dalai Lama's example.[40] Again, his approach to dialogue is personal, positive and profound.

38   'Dialogues,' Mind and Life Institute, accessed 31st July, 2012, http://www.mindandlife. org/dialogues.

39   Jacobs, ed, *Masters of Wisdom: His Holiness the Dalai Lama*, 70 ff.

40   Chopra, 'Gentle Bridges and Golden Seeds: the Dalai Lama's Dialogues with Science,' in *Understanding the Dalai Lama*, 146-158.

Theory and Practice

Where dialogue is concerned, the Dalai Lama is a practitioner more than a theorist, and the principles explored above, are, to a large extent, drawn out of accounts of his practice. They can readily be channelled back into practice by other practitioners sufficiently inspired by the Dalai Lama's example to try to adopt them. Adopting some of the aspects of the Dalai Lama's approach, such as utter compassion towards 'enemies', and real openness to presence and friendship, seems a tall order; they depend on qualities of character that are impressive partly because they are rare. It is worth citing the Dalai Lama here: 'Let me emphasize that it is within your power, given patience and time, to develop [impartial] compassion.'[41] Many of his talks and writings give practical advice, relevant to people of all faiths and none, on developing the kind of compassion which seems to make his presence in dialogue so inspiring and valuable.[42] He suggests ways of thinking about compassion and the emotions which obstruct it, introduces helpful meditations and advises on building the development of compassion into one's daily routine.[43] Karen Armstrong, whose approach to dialogue is discussed in this volume, gives comparable guidance on developing compassion in her *Twelve Steps to a Compassionate Life*.[44]

The Dalai Lama has engaged in innumerable dialogues of one kind or another. Here, we will limit ourselves to looking at the form and key characteristics of three particular projects to which he has contributed.

We have already mentioned above the 'Mind and Life' dialogues which the Dalai Lama has been part of for over twenty-five years. Initiated by cognitive neuroscientist Francisco Varela, entrepreneur Adam Engle and the Dalai Lama, they began as private conversations with the Dalai Lama and small groups of scientists but have gradually grown. They have looked at topics ranging from destructive emotions to cosmology. A core concern of the dialogues is to introduce scientists to Buddhist practitioners' first hand insights into the mind, and to help Buddhists explore the potential of science to analyse and maximise the benefits of their practices. Through these mutually beneficial encounters and related research and publications,

---

41   Compassion and the Individual,' official website of the Office of His Holiness the 14th Dalai Lama, accessed 27th July, 2012, http://www.dalailama.com/messages/compassion.

42   See, for example, *Awakening the Mind, Lightening the Heart* (London: Thorsons, 1997), *The Little Book of Wisdom* (London: Rider, 2000) and *Ancient Wisdom, Modern World: Ethics for the New Millennium* (London: Little, Brown and Company, 1999).

43   See, for example, Tenzin Gyatso, *Ancient Wisdom, Modern World: Ethics for the New Millennium*, ch.8.

44   Karen Armstrong, *Twelve Steps to a Compassionate Life,* London: Bodley Head, 2011.

the Mind and Life Institute which runs the dialogues ultimately seeks 'to relieve human suffering and advance well-being.'[45]

Journalist Swati Chopra's account of the 2001 Mind and Life dialogue reveals something of the spirit in which the dialogues are conducted. The dialogue lasted five days, with scientists giving presentations in the mornings and the Dalai Lama in the afternoons. The Dalai Lama's impressive grasp of scientific matters and great eagerness to understand fostered a tone of serious, positive enquiry. His ability to look at an issue from the scientist's point of view enables him, Chopra notes, 'to form the gentle bridges that enable one to reach out to the other.'[46] When the dialogue between two very different systems reached dead ends respectful attitudes were maintained. Chopra notes a lack of competitiveness, 'perhaps because of the privacy of the meetings that frees the scientists from their constituencies, and perhaps because there is an unsaid agreement not to hurt, to be gentle with one another.' The Dalai Lama's laughing facilitation was able to 'ease things along' at difficult moments.[47] Individual discussions with the Dalai Lama helped to break the ice with sceptical scientists new to the experience, and the dialogue continued informally during travel and at guesthouses. This complex, challenging dialogue was made feasible and valuable by the respectful, human approach encouraged by the Dalai Lama's example.

The Dalai Lama has also been a key force in the development of profound, personal interfaith dialogue among monks and nuns. Following the success of the John Main Seminar which we mentioned above, it was extended into a three year programme of dialogues called 'The Way of Peace.' Maintaining a focus on shared meditation, it comprised a moving joint pilgrimage to the site of the Buddha's enlightenment, a retreat at a Christian monastery and a seminar in Northern Ireland promoting healing and friendship through dialogue.[48] The Dalai Lama has also participated in two major dialogues (the Gethsemani Encounters) with Monastic Interreligious Dialogue, a United States-based organisation of Catholic monks and nuns committed to dialogue. Sister Mary Margaret Funk comments as follows on the intensity and profundity of the dialogue at the first event in 1996:

---

45   'Values, Vision, Mission and Strategy,' Mind and Life Institute, accessed 31st July, 2012, http://www.mindandlife.org/about/mission/.

46   Chopra, 'Gentle Bridges and Golden Seeds: the Dalai Lama's Dialogues with Science,' in *Understanding the Dalai Lama*, 150.

47   Chopra, 'Gentle Bridges and Golden Seeds: the Dalai Lama's Dialogues with Science,' in *Understanding the Dalai Lama*, 152.

48   'Interview: Laurence Freeman comments on the friendship with Dalai Lama, World Community of Christian Meditation,' The World Community for Christian Meditation, accessed 31st July, 2012, http://www.wccm.org/content/interview-laurence-freeman-comments-friendship-dalai-lama.

Each of the different aspects of the week – the talks, the dialogues, dyad encounters [sharing in pairs], rituals, periods of meditation, meals – were parts of an integrated whole… There were no "safe places," as Fr. Thomas Baima put it, into which one could retreat—we plunged into a deep engagement with each other and remained in that encounter for the full week. …there was a sense that we were not there just for ourselves; but were in fact living and working together for the benefit of humankind.[49]

The Dalai Lama has also been an enthusiastic supporter of a related inter-monastic hospitality exchange between small groups of Tibetan monks and nuns and Catholic monks and nuns in the United States. The groups visit a number of communities during the exchange, staying at each for between one and four weeks and entering fully into the religious life of each. Another of the Dalai Lama's dialogue partners, Brother Wayne Teasdale, comments that the quality of the dialogue at the Gethsemani Encounters owes much to the profound connections that had been made between participants in the exchange visits.[50]

The Dalai Lama's Foundation for Universal Responsibility, established with the Nobel Peace Prize which he received in 1989, contributes to dialogue in both the interfaith and conflict resolution contexts. One of its notable interfaith initiatives is its youth interfaith pilgrimages in India, in which young people of different faiths develop deeper interfaith understanding and appreciation through a shared 'experiential journey'. They visit and stay at different religious communities and spiritual centres, learning from religious teachers, attending religious services and taking part in discussions and lectures.[51] True to the Dalai Lama's approach to interfaith dialogue, this project fosters interfaith learning through personal encounters, between the young people and with the religious teachers they meet, and through firsthand experience of different religious traditions.[52]

Another initiative of the Foundation is Women in Security, Conflict Management and Peace (WISCOMP), 'a South Asian research and training initiative, which facilitates the leadership of women in the areas of peace, security and international

---

49   'Gethsemani I: Events,' Monastic Interreligious Dialogue, accessed 31st July, 2012, http://monasticdialog.com/a.php?id=627.

50   Wayne Teasdale, 'The Ocean of Wisdom,' in *Understanding the Dalai Lama*, 94.

51   'Interfaith Confluence,' Foundation for Universal Responsibility, accessed 31st July, 2012, http://www.furhhdl.org/interfaith.

52   'Youth Interfaith Pilgrimage Brochure,' Foundation for Universal Responsibility, accessed 31st July, 2012, http://issuu.com/furhhdl/docs/youth_interfaith-pilgrimage-2012?mode=window&viewMode=doublePage.

affairs.'[53] Its projects supporting grass roots peace building, notably in Jammu and Kashmir, have included workshops on dialogue processes in conflict situations, as well as dialogues about local challenges bringing together people of different gender, culture, religion and profession.[54]

As we have seen, the Dalai Lama's ideal of personal, positive and profound dialogue is being carried forward in a range of groundbreaking initiatives to which he himself contributes or has contributed.

53   'Mission Statement,' WISCOMP, accessed 31st July, 2012, http://www.wiscomp.org/ mission.asp.

54   'Dialogue Processes,' WISCOMP, accessed 31st July, 2012, http://www.wiscomp.org/ jandk-dialogue.asp.

Questions for Reflection

1. The Dalai Lama encourages people of different faiths to pray and meditate together and to visit one another's holy sites. He is known for visiting and participating in the rituals of other traditions.

   a. What are the potential benefits of such participatory dialogue?

   b. Is there a point at which participating in the religious life of other traditions might become problematic? Where does that point lie?

2. What is the place of silence in dialogue? How might you use silence at an interfaith or intercultural community dialogue event?

3. The Dalai Lama considers that sensitive issues, such as those between a religious or ethnic minority and the majority, need to be stated and explored openly.

   a. Do you agree?

   b. When should we eat, meditate or work together and when should we talk about sensitive issues?

4. Through decades of nonviolence and attempts at dialogue, the Dalai Lama has not achieved a satisfactory solution on Tibet.

   a. Is dialogue sometimes just not the answer?

   b. What would be an acceptable substitute, or supplement?

Bibliography

Armstrong, Karen. *Twelve Steps to a Compassionate Life*. London: Bodley Head, 2011.

Chopra, Swati. 'Gentle Bridges and Golden Seeds: the Dalai Lama's Dialogues with Science.' In *Understanding the Dalai Lama*, edited by Rajiv Mehtotra, 146-158. London: Penguin Books, 2006.

Craig, Mary. 'A Very Human Human Being.' In *Understanding the Dalai Lama*, edited by Rajiv Mehtotra, 70-76. London: Penguin Books, 2006.

Forsthoefel, Thomas A. ed. *The Dalai Lama: Essential Writings*. Maryknoll, New York: Orbis Books, 2008.

Foundation for Universal Responsibility. Accessed 31st July, 2012. http://www.furhhdl.org.

Gyatso, Tenzin, the Fourteenth Dalai Lama. *Ancient Wisdom, Modern World: Ethics for the New Millennium*. London: Little, Brown and Company, 1999.

Gyatso, Tenzin, the Fourteenth Dalai Lama. *Awakening the Mind, Lightening the Heart*. London: Thorsons, 1997.

Gyatso, Tenzin, the Fourteenth Dalai Lama. *My Spiritual Autobiography*. London: Rider, 2010.

Gyatso, Tenzin, the Fourteenth Dalai Lama. *The Good Heart: a Buddhist Perspective on the Teachings of Jesus*. Somerville, MA: Wisdom Publications, 1996.

Gyatso, Tenzin, the Fourteenth Dalai Lama and Matthew Bunson. *The Little Book of Wisdom*. London: Rider, 2000.

Jacobs, Alan ed. *Masters of Wisdom: His Holiness the Dalai Lama: Infinite Compassion for an Imperfect World*. London: Watkins Publishing, 2011.

Mind and Life Institute. Accessed 31st July, 2012. http://www.mindandlife.org.

Monastic Interreligious Dialogue. Accessed 31st July, 2012. http://monasticdialog.com.

Office of His Holiness the 14th Dalai Lama. Accessed 31st July, 2012. http://www.dalailama.com.

Office of His Holiness the 14th Dalai Lama. 'Non Violence and Ethical Values.' Accessed 15th January, 2013. http://www.dalailama.com/webcasts/post/252-non-violence-and-ethical-values.

Puri, Bharati. 'Universal Responsibility in the Dalai Lama's World View.' In *Understanding the Dalai Lama*, edited by Rajiv Mehtotra, 105-117. London: Penguin Books, 2006.

Rajiv Mehrotra ed. *Understanding the Dalai Lama*. London: Penguin Books, 2006.

Ram, Senthil. 'The Dalai Lama as a Political Strategist.' In *Understanding the Dalai Lama*, edited by Rajiv Mehtotra, 159-174. London: Penguin Books, 2006.

Teasdale, Brother Wayne. 'The Ocean of Wisdom.' In *Understanding the Dalai Lama*, edited by Rajiv Mehtotra, 85-98. London: Penguin Books, 2006.

Thurman, Robert. *Why the Dalai Lama Matters: his Act of Truth as the Solution for*

China, Tibet and the World. New York: Atria Books/Hillsboro, Oregon: Beyond Words Publishing, 2008.

WISCOMP (Women in Security Conflict Management and Peace). Accessed 31st July, 2012. http://www.wiscomp.org.

World Community of Christian Meditation. 'Interview: Laurence Freeman comments on the friendship with Dalai Lama, World Community of Christian Meditation.' Accessed 31st July, 2012. http://www.wccm.org/content/interview-laurence-freeman-comments-friendship-dalai-lama.

Recommended Reading

The Dalai Lama's Works:

Forsthoefel, Thomas A. ed. *The Dalai Lama: Essential Writings*. Maryknoll, New York: Orbis Books, 2008.

Gyatso, Tenzin, the Fourteenth Dalai Lama. *Ancient Wisdom, Modern World: Ethics for the New Millennium*. London: Little, Brown and Company, 1999.

Gyatso, Tenzin, the Fourteenth Dalai Lama. *Awakening the Mind, Lightening the Heart*. London: Thorsons, 1997.

Gyatso, Tenzin, the Fourteenth Dalai Lama. *Beyond Religion: Ethics for a Whole World*. London: Rider, 2012.

Gyatso, Tenzin, the Fourteenth Dalai Lama. *My Spiritual Autobiography*. London: Rider, 2010.

Gyatso, Tenzin, the Fourteenth Dalai Lama. *The Good Heart: a Buddhist Perspective on the Teachings of Jesus*. Somerville, MA: Wisdom Publications, 1996.

Gyatso, Tenzin, the Fourteenth Dalai Lama and Matthew Bunson. *The Little Book of Wisdom*. London: Rider, 2000.

Jacobs, Alan ed. *Masters of Wisdom: His Holiness the Dalai Lama: Infinite Compassion for an Imperfect World*. London: Watkins Publishing, 2011.

Office of His Holiness the 14th Dalai Lama. Accessed 31st July, 2012. http://www.dalailama.com.

Commentary:

Rajiv Mehrotra, ed. *Understanding the Dalai Lama*. London: Penguin Books, 2006.

Thurman, Robert. *Why the Dalai Lama Matters: his Act of Truth as the Solution for China, Tibet and the World*. New York: Atria Books/Hillsboro, Oregon: Beyond Words Publishing, 2008.

Practical Applications:

Foundation for Universal Responsibility. Accessed 31st July, 2012. http://www.furhhdl.org

Mind and Life Institute. Accessed 31st July, 2012.
http://www.mindandlife.org

Monastic Interreligious Dialogue. Accessed 31st July, 2012.
http://monasticdialog.com

WISCOMP (Women in Security Conflict Management and Peace). Accessed 31st
July, 2012. http://www.wiscomp.org.

Jürgen Habermas

Biographical Introduction

Jürgen Habermas is a highly influential German social theorist. He is widely regarded as one of the most important social theorists of his era.[1] His ambitious, comprehensive theories range widely over the areas of sociology, philosophy of language, ethics and politics.

He was born in Düsseldorf in 1929. The Second World War ended when he was fifteen. He was significantly marked by the shocking realisation of the atrocities that had been committed by the Nazis and the extent of the moral collapse of the German political system. His disillusionment with his first big intellectual influence, the philosopher Martin Heidegger, stemmed from Heidegger's failure to express regret for his active support of Nazism. His criticism of Heidegger marked the beginning of his ongoing practice of speaking out on political issues that 'irritate' him, from German Federal policy to the Iraq and Kosovo wars. A true public intellectual, he has sometimes been called Germany's 'intellectual conscience.'[2]

Habermas initially studied philosophy at the universities of Gottingen, Zurich and Bonn. After gaining his doctorate he went on to work with the philosophers Theodor W. Adorno and Max Horkheimer at the Institute for Social Research at the University of Frankfurt am Main. There he developed a strong interest in Karl Marx, although he was never an uncritical Marxist. He returned to Frankfurt as a professor in 1982 after periods in Heidelberg and Starnberg.

Habermas, like Adorno and Horkheimer, belongs to the Frankfurt School of social theory. Adopting elements of Marxism, this group of thinkers has critiqued modern society and its tendency towards domination and the single-minded pursuit of material goals.[3] Habermas's outlook is less pessimistic than that of his predecessors, partly, it seems, because he was so young at the end of the War, and has since witnessed that 'things really got rather better.'[4] Adorno and Horkheimer

---

1   William Outhwaite, *Habermas* (Cambridge: Polity Press, 2004), 6; James Gordon Finlayson, *Habermas: a Very Short Introduction* (New York: OUP, 2006), Preface.

2   Outhwaite, *Habermas,* 6 f.

3   'Jürgen Habermas – Biography,' The European Graduate School, accessed 13th June, 2012, http://www.egs.edu/library/juergen-habermas/biography/.

4   Cited in Arie Brand, *The Force of Reason: An Introduction to Habermas's Theory of Communicative Action* (Sydney: Allen and Unwin, 1990), xi.

considered that as societies develop, becoming more complex and more rational, they inevitably move towards weaker social bonds and loss of meaning.[5] Habermas denies the inevitability of this process. Modern capitalist societies have, he agrees, become dominated by a single-minded concern to achieve individual goals. However, he insists that the kind of rationality through which we pursue individual ends is not the only form of rationality we possess. In different conditions societies might develop in a much more balanced way, giving more attention to other forms of rationality.[6]

Human beings are, he holds, equipped with *communicative* rationality, which allows us to establish understanding and consensus, and to coordinate our actions without coercion in a way acceptable to all involved. He calls this reasoned coordination *communicative action*. His exploration of this coordination, and the sort of discourse that makes it possible, are a key part of his great work *The Theory of Communicative Action*.[7]

Habermas's theory of communicative action is of particular interest to us here, as are his explorations of the conditions required for the proper functioning of communicative action.

---

5   They share this outlook with Max Weber, a great pioneer of social science who died in 1920.

6   Brand, *The Force of Reason*, x.

7   Jürgen Habermas, *The Theory of Communicative Action*, Vol, I trans. Thomas McCarthy (London: Heinemann, 1984); *The Theory of Communicative Action* Vol 2, trans. Thomas McCarthy (Boston: Beacon Press, 1987). Original German: *Theorie des kommunikativen Handelns* (1981).

Thought on Dialogue

Habermas's main concern in the area of communication is not with dialogue per se but with 'communicative action' and the discourse involved in such action. Because communicative action is related to the search for consensus and the coordination of action, it has a special relevance for practitioners of 'deliberation,' which is widely conceived as being more focused upon these concerns than the more open-ended 'dialogue'. One recent definition describes deliberation as follows: "'a problem-solving form of discourse, which involves problem analysis, setting priorities, establishing evaluative criteria, identifying and weighing alternative solutions", and which, at least in aspiration, "aims toward a reasoned consensus."'[8] However, even for those practitioners and theorists of dialogue who are deliberately *un*concerned with consensus and action, Habermas's vision of honest, non-coercive communication still provides a number of relevant ideals to which to aspire.

It is worth setting Habermas's ideals of communication in the context of his career-long concern with the proper functioning of democracy. Real democracy, Habermas considers, is secured by deliberation in the 'public sphere', that is, in all those forums in which citizens engage in unrestricted discussion of 'matters of general interest'.[9] The public sphere may include parliaments and political associations, pubs and coffee houses, newspapers and journals. Habermas, in his 1962 work *The Structural Transformation of the Public Sphere*[10], associated the emergence of the public sphere with the rationalist thought of the Enlightenment and the democratic American and French revolutions of the 18th century. In this era it became possible for citizens to have an impact on politics via the formation of public opinion through public discussion.[11] [12] Challenge or support from the public sphere provided balance and

---

8   P. Levine et al, 'Future Directions for Public Deliberation,' *Journal of Public Deliberation*, 1, no. 1 (2005), cited in Ute Kelly and Lisa Cumming, *Civil Society Supporting Dialogue and Deliberation* (Carnegie UK Trust, 2010).

9   Jürgen Habermas, 'The Public Sphere: An Encyclopedia Article,' in *Critical Theory and Society: A Reader*, ed. Stephen Eric Bronner and Douglas Kellner (New York: Routledge, 1989), 136.

10   Jürgen Habermas, *The Structural Transformation of the Public Sphere* (Cambridge, Mass: MIT Press, 1989). Original German title: *Strukturwandel der Öffentlichkeit. Untersuchungen zu einer Kategorie der bürgerlichen Gesellschaft* (1962).

11   Douglas Kellner, 'Habermas, the Public Sphere, and Democracy: A Critical Intervention,' University of California, LA, Graduate School of Education and Information Studies, 2000, 1f. Accessed 20th Mar, 2013, http://pages.gseis.ucla.edu/faculty/kellner/essays/habermaspublicspheredemocracy.pdf.

12   We see Daniel Yankelovich take a similar approach to the roles of discussion and public opinion in democracy in our chapter on his work in this volume.

guidance for the state administration by providing or withdrawing legitimation.[13]

Habermas considers that the public sphere is not allowed to play such a role in contemporary societies dominated by the social welfare state and corporate capitalism. In such societies the public sphere is constrained and controlled rather than complemented by the state and by the media. Ordinary citizens lose their active role in democracy and small elites control society. Habermas has come to place his hope for the revival of properly functioning democracy, not in any unpredictable historical factors, but in the intrinsic human capacity for communicative action, which is the main focus of this chapter.[14]

We will now proceed to look further at what Habermas means by 'communicative action', focusing at his exploration of the idea in his key work *The Theory of Communicative Action*.[15] We will then explore the set of conditions he lays down for the proper functioning of 'argumentation' which is an important kind of discourse related to communicative action. Finally we will take a look at Habermas's view of the role of these kinds of human interaction in society.

In communicative action, those involved seek a common understanding of their situation, and on the basis of this, 'harmonize their plans of actions' so that the actions of each will be acceptable to all.[16] Consensus is achieved without coercion, threat or manipulation, through the use of honest, rational discussion. When a claim made by one of the participants is disputed, the participants take a step back from the immediate concern with action and explore the claim in order to achieve common understanding. This kind of exploration, at one remove from the concern with action, is called 'argumentation'.[17]

---

13   Habermas, 'Further Reflections on the Public Sphere,' in *Habermas and the Public Sphere*, ed. Craig Calhoun (Cambridge: The MIT Press, 1992), 452.

14   Kellner, 'Habermas, the Public Sphere, and Democracy: A Critical Intervention,' 3 f, 10 ff.

15   Habermas, *The Theory of Communicative Action*, Vol 1, 10.

16   Habermas, *The Theory of Communicative Action*, Vol 1, 10.

17   Argumentation is not same thing as communicative action; it is the form of verbal interaction through which people explore and resolve claims that are raised in communicative action and then disputed: Habermas, *Moral Consciousness and Communicative Action*, trans. C. Lenhardt and S.W. Nicholsen (Cambridge MA: MIT Press, 1990), 87. Original German: *Moralbewusstsein und kommunikatives Handeln* (1983). Communicative action frequently relies on verbal interaction, or 'speech acts', but is not identified with them; it is a matter of the rational coordination of action: Habermas, *The Theory of Communicative Action*, Vol. I, 295.

According to Habermas, human language is characterised by the inherent effort towards consensus. Animals such as chimpanzees can, it has been shown, form propositions and express feelings through language.[18] The distinctive characteristic of *human* language is its use in seeking a shared understanding of the situation and coordinating actions accordingly. Habermas writes that 'with the first sentence used the intention to reach a general and uncompelled consensus is pronounced unmistakeably.'[19]

Habermas claims that just by speaking in the context of communicative action the speaker is implicitly claiming to live up to certain standards, and expressing the expectation that others will do the same. Just by speaking, she is implying that what she says makes sense; that it is true, reflecting how things actually are; that it is right, that is, it is in accordance with moral norms; and that it is sincere. These claims to truth, rightness, and sincerity relate to the different spheres of human experience: the objective world of measurable facts; the social world of norms of human behaviour and interaction and the subjective world of the individual's private experience. We can criticise the validity of what somebody says on any of these levels. Habermas gives the example of a professor asking a student to get him a glass of water. The student might challenge the request by noting that there is, objectively, no water available; she might criticise the request's moral acceptability, saying that she is being treated like a servant; or she might question the request's sincerity, suspecting that the professor does not even want a drink.[20] In communicative action, speech should be true, right and sincere.

Habermas contrasts communicative action, which is oriented towards understanding, with action oriented towards success. Action oriented towards success involves a person fixing on a personal goal, working out what he needs to do in order to succeed, and proceeding to do this. Sometimes this kind of action involves influencing the decisions of another rational person in order to further one's personal goal; this kind of success-oriented action is called 'strategic action.' Habermas underlines what makes communicative action different from such strategic action as follows: 'In communicative action participants are not primarily oriented to their own individual successes; they pursue their individual goals under the condition that they can harmonize their plans of action on the basis of common situation definitions.'[21] For Habermas, reaching understanding is what human speech is inherently *for*. Reaching understanding is its inherent goal, or *telos*.

---

18   Brand, *The Force of Reason*, 11.

19   Habermas, *Toward a Rational Society*, trans J. J. Shapiro (Boston: Beacon, 1970), 163, cited in Brand, *The Force of Reason*, 11.

20   Outhwaite, *Habermas*, 39; Brand, *The Force of Reason*, 16.

21   Habermas, *The Theory of Communicative Action*, Vol. I, 286.

Accordingly, Habermas sees speech used strategically as *parasitic* on speech used in reaching understanding.[22] Strategic uses of speech distort its inherent purpose.[23]

Some examples may provide a better picture of strategic and communicative action. If a person holds a gun to my head and says, 'Give me your money or I'll shoot!' his words and actions are clearly oriented towards his own project of becoming slightly richer, not towards shared understanding and the rational coordination of our actions on that basis. He is not making claims to truth, rightness or sincerity and asking me to bear them in mind in planning my next actions; he is relying on the threat of force.[24] Strategic action depends on threats of force and promises of reward.

In some cases strategic action is not so open in its intentions. If my housemate says to me, 'I am just taking out the rubbish for the third time in a row,' her words take the form of the simple communication of a fact, a contribution to understanding. However, she intends, through her tone, and her reference to 'the third time', to make me feel guilty and thereby influence my behaviour; her unstated intention is that next time, to avoid further guilt, I make sure I take out the rubbish. This is an example of concealed strategic action.

In communicative action, the persuasive force of a person's speech does not come from the power of threat or promise, but from a claim to validity. In speech oriented to understanding the speaker implies that what he says is true, right and sincere and, further, implies that if asked to do so he will somehow demonstrate this. When a flight attendant says to me, 'I am hereby requiring you to stop smoking' I understand that she is appealing to a set of regulations, not simply to her own will or to the threat of force. I am motivated to stop smoking because I recognise that she has legitimate grounds for telling me to do so.[25]

Having explored the way in which Habermas contrasts communicative action with strategic action, let us take a closer look at the process of argumentation, through which disputed claims raised by communicative action are explored.[26] Habermas

---

22   Habermas, *The Theory of Communicative Action*, Vol. I, 287.

23   Brand, *The Force of Reason*, 16.

24   Habermas, *The Theory of Communicative Action*, Vol. I, 300.

25   Habermas, *The Theory of Communicative Action*, Vol. I. 300.

26   Disputed claims may be claims to truth, to rightness or to sincerity.

provides a set of rules for argumentation in his essay on 'Discourse Ethics'.[27] Habermas holds that these rules are in fact *presuppositions* of argumentation. They are the conditions that must be fulfilled for argumentation to carry on without disruption in an unadulterated form. When we engage in argumentation, while the conditions will never be fulfilled perfectly, we have to assume that they are fulfilled to a reasonable extent. Further, when we participate in argumentation we are in a sense 'signing up' to the ideal of argumentation in its pure form, and to the conditions which make it possible. In some of his writings Habermas refers to the situation defined by the presuppositions of argumentation as the 'ideal speech situation.'[28] He stresses that the presuppositions listed in 'Discourse Ethics' are only an incomplete sketch.

The first three rules outline the conditions required for the arguments made in argumentation to be clear and coherent. These rules are:[29]

1.1 No speaker may contradict himself.

1.2 Every speaker who applies predicate *F* to object *A* must be prepared to apply *F* to all other objects resembling *A* in all relevant aspects.

For instance, if I say, 'James is untrustworthy – he was involved in that publicity scam,' I cannot then claim that John, who was involved in the same scam, is trustworthy.

1.3 Different speakers may not use the same expression with different meanings.

If I use the phrase, 'the old man' to mean sometimes my husband and sometimes my father, no one will be sure who I am talking about at any given time; I have to be consistent in how I use the phrase.

---

27 Habermas, 'Discourse Ethics and its Basis in Action Theory,' in Habermas, *Moral Consciousness and Communicative Action*, trans. C. Lenhardt and S.W. Nicholsen (Cambridge MA: MIT Press, 1990), 87 ff. The conditions he gives are taken from R. Alexy's system of presuppositions, based on an elaboration of some of Habermas's earlier writing on the same theme: R. Alexy, 'Eine Theorie des praktischen Diskurses,' in W. Oelmiller, ed., *Normenbegrindung, Normdurchsetzung* (Paderborn, 1978).

28 For example, in his 1973 essay 'Wahrheitstheorien,' 211ff. He refers to this essay in *Moral Consciousness and Communicative Action*, 88.

29 Habermas, *Moral Consciousness and Communicative Action*, 87 ff. Note that Habermas stresses that the presuppositions listed in 'Discourse Ethics' are only an incomplete sketch.

The next rules ensure that argumentation can fulfil its function of identifying truth and establishing genuine shared understanding.

> 2.1 Every speaker must only assert only what he really believes.

> 2.2 A person who disputes a proposition or norm not under discussion must provide a reason for wanting to do so.

> Changing the subject and focusing on unrelated claims will not help us reach agreement about the claim under discussion.

Since argumentation is about establishing *rationally motivated* agreement about a disputed claim, it 'rules out all external or internal coercion other than the force of the better argument and... neutralizes all motives other than the cooperative search for truth.'[30] The following presuppositions underline the requirements of free participation and expression.

> 3.1 Every subject with the competence to speak and act is allowed to take part in a discourse.

> 3.2 a. Everyone is allowed to question any assertion whatever.

> b. Everyone is allowed to introduce any assertion whatever into the discourse.

> c. Everyone is allowed to express his attitudes, desires and needs.

Habermas recognises that the shining ideal of argumentation outlined here is, to say the least, challenging to implement in the real world. Such forms of discourse, he writes, 'resemble islands threatened with inundation in a sea of practice where the pattern of consensual conflict resolution is by no means the dominant one. The means of reaching agreement are repeatedly thrust aside by the instruments of force.'[31] He notes that there is a place for the institutionalisation of some forms of discourse, bringing them closer to the ideal by laying down rules on how they should be conducted.[32]

In *The Theory of Communicative Action*, communicative action is explored in the context of a broader theory of society, and of how society reproduces itself as generations come and go. There are two elements to society's reproduction:

---

30   Habermas, *Moral Consciousness and Communicative Action*, 88 f.

31   Habermas, *Moral Consciousness and Communicative Action*, 106.

32   Habermas, *Moral Consciousness and Communicative Action*, 92.

material reproduction and symbolic reproduction. While material reproduction is the constant manufacture of the physical necessities of human life, symbolic reproduction is the reproduction of what Habermas calls the 'lifeworld', which consists of social rules and norms, culture and personality. Habermas understands culture as the shared knowledge which provides the basis of mutual understanding, and personality as the individual's ability to speak, act and take part effectively in communicative action.[33] While strategic action can effectively achieve material reproduction, the symbolic reproduction of the lifeworld demands communicative action. Without communicative action we cannot educate the next generation, incorporate new ideas and insights into our collective knowledge and ways of life,[34] or bring up our children as competent members of society. Further, of course, communicative action in the public sphere is the very stuff of democracy.[35]

Habermas considers that in modern capitalist societies communicative action, and thus our ability to reproduce the lifeworld, is seriously inhibited. In the course of their history these societies have undergone a gradual process of rationalisation, increasingly subjecting common assumptions and practices to evaluation and criticism, and developing ever more sophisticated understandings of the world and ever more elaborate systems for society's reproduction. Ultimately societies became too complex to be managed entirely by the lifeworld's processes of discussion and reasoned consensus. Through power and money the systems of state and market coordinated society in simpler but more coercive terms. Laws in our contemporary societies are now widely experienced as requirements imposed from above, rather than as expressions of moral consensus. The market seems as unpredictable as the weather, rather than being a readily comprehensible mechanism of human interaction. Power and money and the systems in which they operate are dominated by strategic action, rather than communicative action.

The problems of contemporary capitalist societies lie in the fact that money, power and the strategic action bound up with them have become so pervasive and powerful that no sphere of life seems able to remain independent of them. Those

---

33 Brand, *The Force of Reason*, 35 f.

34 Reproduction of the lifeworld does not just involve passing on culture and knowledge but also the processing and incorporation of new ideas. See Thomas L. Jacobson and J. Douglas Storey, 'Development Communication and Participation: Applying Habermas to a Case Study of Population Programs in Nepal,' *Communication Theory* 14, no. 2 (May 2004): 104ff. Jacobsen and Storey cite Habermas, *Autonomy and Solidarity*, London: Verso, 1992.

35 Bent Flyvberg, 'Habermas and Foucault: Thinkers for Civil Society?' *The British Journal of Sociology*, 49, no. 2 (June 1998): 212ff; Kellner, 'Habermas, the Public Sphere and Democracy: A Critical Intervention,' 1 ff.

areas of life which can only be reproduced through communicative action are increasingly subject to the impersonal, bureaucratic regulation through which the state and the market function. Habermas calls this the colonisation of the lifeworld. Modern culture simply does not have the coherence to see the big picture of what is happening and to counter it. This is because knowledge has become fragmented through the development of expert cultures, such as scientific fields and law, which fail to communicate effectively with one another or with the general public.[36]

In Habermas's view, the social ills resulting from this 'colonisation' are not inevitable results of society's development and rationalisation. The inherent human propensity for reasoned consensus and coordination offers the possibility of the development of a more balanced society.[37] Without going into details, Habermas suggests that organisations could potentially be reformed to make them more oriented to communicative action and the proper functioning of the public sphere.[38] Social movements and other agencies sufficiently independent of the ailing capitalist system to criticise its bases have an important role to play in reviving the role of public sphere deliberation.[39]

For Habermas, communicative action, and the rational, non-coercive discussion and argumentation through which it is achieved, are an integral part of what it is to be human. They are indispensable for the survival of the crucial elements of society that Habermas calls the lifeworld, and they are the foundation of democracy. They are also the only answer to the ills of modern society.

---

36   Brand, *The Force of Reason*, 41 ff.

37   Brand, *The Force of Reason*, 10 ff.

38   Jürgen Habermas, 'The Public Sphere: An Encyclopedia Article,' 142; Kellner, 'Habermas, the Public Sphere, and Democracy: A Critical Intervention,' 6.

39   David Oki Ahearn, 'Urban Empowerment as Public Participation: the Atlanta Project and Jürgen Habermas's Theory of Communicative Action,' *Annual of the Society of Christian Ethics* 20 (2000): 353.

Theory and Practice

As we have seen above, Habermas has a lively concern with 'practice'; he is concerned with social and political issues, and sees communicative action and the related forms of speech as playing a key role in addressing the ills of modernity.

But how much real guidance can Habermas offer those involved in the practice of dialogue and deliberation in different fields? One of the criticisms commonly levelled at Habermas is that his theories are too idealistic and removed from the complex realities of human life. His contemporary, the French philosopher Michel Foucault, argued that his vision of non-coercive, communicative action fails to recognise that *all* human dealings are coloured by inequality, and the power struggles and strategic action that accompany it.[40] Critics have also noted that Habermas's model idealises a rather Western model of cool, rational interaction.[41] Does his work, then, have anything to offer practice in an immensely diverse and deeply unequal world?

A look at the range of articles on the practical application of Habermas's theory suggests that, in fact, it does.

Certainly, as indeed Habermas recognises,[42] there will be discrepancies between the model he provides and real-life situations of deliberation. We see this in David Oki Ahearn's examination of the model in relation to the Atlanta Project, a large-scale community empowerment programme in Atlanta in the 1990's. Clearly the interactions of the stakeholders and volunteers involved in this programme did not always follow the sequence implied in Habermas's model: rational discourse, consensus, action. Sometimes joint action in which each participant acted for their own ends resulted in trust that then made more meaningful discourse possible.[43] Ahearn also notes that Habermas's view that the world of business is characterised by a lack of communicative action and that voluntary organisations are best placed to revive it is not necessarily supported by experience; in the Atlanta Project the businesspeople taking part in the project often had the skills to provide strong models of genuine communicative action.[44]

---

40   See Flyvbjerg, 'Habermas and Foucault: Thinkers for Civil Society?'

41   Jacobson and Storey, 'Development Communication and Participation,' 101.

42   Habermas, *Moral Consciousness and Communicative Action,* 105 f. See 'Thought on Dialogue' section above.

43   David Oki Ahearn, 'Urban Empowerment as Public Participation,' 357.

44   Ahearn, 'Urban Empowerment as Public Participation,' 355.

Nevertheless, Ahearn notes that Habermas proved 'an insightful guide' in another area. His exploration of the isolation of modern expert cultures shed light on the difficulties faced by community empowerment organisations seeking to draw on the knowledge of experts without allowing them to dominate the conversation.[45] Ahearn is not alone in finding certain of Habermas's theoretical insights of practical help in managing and facilitating deliberative processes. Practitioners in a range of fields draw on Habermas's insights. Some go further, making his concept of communicative action a model for practice and a framework for its evaluation.

Thomas L. Jacobsen and J. Douglas Storey are among those who employ Habermas's theory in this way. Their field is development communication, and they refer to a case study of a population programme in Nepal which attempted to use a participatory approach in educating citizens about family planning. While development communication programmes increasingly seek a 'participatory' approach, the lack of clear definitions makes it difficult to analyse these programmes and evaluate their success. Jacobsen and Storey find that Habermas's theory of communicative action helps to fill this gap: 'the conceptual framework of validity claims, reciprocal expectations, and the symmetrical distribution of opportunities to contribute in discussion, offer an analysis of participatory communication that is more complete than any other approach to participation.'[46]

Jacobsen and Storey consider different parts of the Nepalese population programme in relation to Habermas's ideal, from mass media campaigns to communication workshops for health professionals. Referring to the ideals of honest, uninhibited communication and the free participation of everyone concerned, they consider whether each initiative can be considered 'participatory.' Although a lot more work would need to be done for Habermas's theory to be used in 'program design, implementation and evaluation' they find it a promising approach.

Habermas's tendency to make a particular Western ideal of rationality *the* standard for human communication does not seem to negate the value of his theory in providing theoretical support to this kind of programme, even in a non-Western context.[47] By underlining the right of everybody to express themselves freely on matters that concern them his theory helps to focus efforts to avoid a situation in which those in power simply coerce the disempowered.

In a very different field, Liv Tveit Walseth and Edvin Schei explain how Habermas's work can fill a gap in theory, thus clarifying and enhancing practice. The

---

45   Ahearn, 'Urban Empowerment as Public Participation,' 364, 366.

46   Jacobsen and Storey, 'Development Communication and Participation,' 106.

47   Jacobsen and Storey, 'Development Communication and Participation,' 101.

deliberative processes with which they are concerned are discussions with patients about how to improve their health through lifestyle changes. They found that the theory can provide valuable guidance both on how to talk, and what to talk about. On the question of what to talk about, they found it very helpful to focus on Habermas's three spheres of experience: the objective world, the social world and the subjective world. They found that Habermas supported and clarified their professional sense of the value of exploring all three of these areas with patients, examining their relationships and their sense of what is right, their emotions and their desires along with medical information and practical circumstances. On the question of how to talk, they highlight the following principles contained in the theory of communicative action: 'equitability; inclusion of the relevant parties; respect; sincerity; consistency; information; opinions and reason; justification and reasoning; reflection upon values and norms and willingness to change one's mind when convinced.'[48] Of course, in the medical context certain adjustments have to be made. For example a doctor-patient relationship is inevitably unequal and this has to be accepted and managed compassionately.[49] The guidance of Habermas's ideal remains valuable.

It has value too, according to Stephen Chilton and Maria Stalzer Wyant Cuzzo, in the context of mediation, where a clash of interests, financial or personal, may make it particularly difficult to maintain a reasonable and fair conversation.[50] Chilton and Cuzzo explain how a professional mediator can work to maintain an approximation of Habermas's set of presuppositions of argumentation, by setting out ground rules at the start of the mediation and challenging participants to observe them during the process. Difficult as this will inevitably be in conflict situations, keeping the ideal firmly in mind may make it possible to maintain some level of respectful relationship even when agreement is impossible.

We have seen that in a selection of contexts involving the practice of deliberation, Habermas's theory has been found to be of value in providing a theoretical framework for analysis and evaluation, and an ideal of reasoned, honest and respectful communication. The ideal may well be practically unattainable, and practitioners of all kinds of deliberation and dialogue undoubtedly need to be aware of the omnipresent inequalities of power that make this so. However, we will

---

48   Liv Tveit Walseth and Edvin Schei, 'Effecting change through dialogue: Habermas' theory of communicative action as a tool in medical lifestyle interventions,' *Medical Health Care and Philosophy* 14 (2011): 85.

49   Walseth and Schei, 'Effecting change through dialogue,' 85.

50   Stephen Chilton and Maria Stalzer Wyant Cuzzo, 'Habermas's Theory of Communicative Action as a Theoretical Framework for Mediation Practice,' *Conflict Resolution Quarterly* 22, no. 3 (Spring 2005): 325-348.

surely make more progress towards fair relationships and effective deliberation by attempting to get close to Habermas's shining ideal than we will by renouncing the challenge.

Questions for Reflection

1. Habermas focuses on forms of communication which aim at consensus. Dialogue thinkers and practitioners often say dialogue is not about consensus. To what extent are Habermas's models of communicative action and argumentation relevant to practitioners of dialogue?

2. Habermas's contemporary, the French philosopher Michel Foucault, argued that his vision of non-coercive, communicative action fails to recognise that *all* human dealings are coloured by inequality, and the power struggles and strategic action that accompany it.

   a. Do you think that Habermas's models of communication are attainable?

   b. Have you experienced anything approaching pure communicative action, or argumentation?

   c. Do Habermas's models at least provide a helpful guiding ideal? Or are they too far removed from reality to do so?

3. Do people need particular skills or qualities to engage properly in communicative action or argumentation? What are they? How might they be cultivated?

4. What measures might help promote something approaching Habermassian communication in a tense community discussion?

5. What kind of initiatives in the public sphere might help restore communicative action to its proper place in society?

6. What kind of institutional reform might contribute toward the same goal?

Bibliography

Ahearn, David Oki. 'Urban Empowerment as Public Participation: the Atlanta Project and Jürgen Habermas's Theory of Communicative Action.' *Annual of the Society of Christian Ethics* 20 (2000): 349-368.

Brand, Arie. *The Force of Reason: An Introduction to Habermas's Theory of Communicative Action.* Sydney: Allen and Unwin, 1990.

Chilton, Stephen, and Maria Stalzer Wyant Cuzzo. 'Habermas's Theory of Communicative Action as a Theoretical Framework for Mediation Practice.' *Conflict Resolution Quarterly* 22, no. 3 (Spring 2005): 325-348.

European Graduate School, The. 'Jürgen Habermas – Biography.' Accessed 13th June, 2012. http://www.egs.edu/library/juergen-habermas/biography/

Finlayson, James Gordon. *Habermas: a Very Short Introduction.* New York: OUP, 2006.

Flyvbjerg, Bent. 'Habermas and Foucault: Thinkers for Civil Society?' *The British Journal of Sociology* 49, no. 2 (June 1998): 210-233.

Habermas, Jürgen. *Autonomy and Solidarity.* London: Verso, 1992.

Habermas, Jürgen. 'Further Reflections on the Public Sphere.' In *Habermas and the Public Sphere*, edited by Craig Calhoun, 421-461. Cambridge: The MIT Press, 1992.

Habermas, Jürgen. *Moral Consciousness and Communicative Action.* Translated by C. Lenhardt and S.W. Nicholsen. Cambridge MA: MIT Press, 1990. First published in German, *Moralbewusstsein und kommunikatives Handeln,* 1983.

Habermas, Jürgen. *Structural Transformation of the Public Sphere.* Cambridge, Mass: MIT Press, 1989. First published in German, *Strukturwandel der Öffentlichkeit. Untersuchungen zu einer Kategorie der bürgerlichen Gesellschaft,*1962.

Habermas, Jürgen. 'The Public Sphere: An Encyclopedia Article.' In *Critical Theory and Society: A Reader*, edited by Stephen Eric Bronner and Douglas Kellner, 136-142. New York: Routledge, 1989.

Habermas, Jürgen. *The Theory of Communicative Action,* Vol. I: *Reason and the Rationalization of Society.* Translated by Thomas McCarthy. London: Heinemann, 1984. First published in German, *Theorie des kommunikativen Handelns,* 1981.

Habermas, Jürgen. *The Theory of Communicative Action,* Vol 2: *Lifeworld and System: A Critique of Functionalist Reason.* Translated by Thomas McCarthy. Boston: Beacon Press, 1987. First published in German, *Theorie des kommunikativen Handelns,* 1981.

Habermas, Jürgen. *Toward a Rational Society.* Translated by J. J. Shapiro. Boston: Beacon, 1970.

Jacobson, Thomas L., and J. Douglas Storey. 'Development Communication and Participation: Applying Habermas to a Case Study of Population Programs in Nepal.' *Communication Theory* 14, no. 2 (May 2004): 99-121.

Kellner, Douglas. 'Habermas, the Public Sphere, and Democracy: A Critical Intervention.' University of California, Los Angeles, Graduate School of Education and Information Studies, 2000. Accessed 20th March, 2013, http://pages.gseis.ucla.edu/faculty/kellner/essays/ habermaspublicspheredemocracy.pdf.

Outhwaite, William. *Habermas.* Cambridge: Polity Press, 2004.

Walseth, Liv Tveit, and Edvin Schei. 'Effecting change through dialogue: Habermas' theory of communicative action as a tool in medical lifestyle interventions.' *Medical Health Care and Philosophy* 14 (2011): 81-90.

Recommended Reading

Habermas's Works:

Habermas, Jürgen. 'Further Reflections on the Public Sphere.' In *Habermas and the Public Sphere*, edited by Craig Calhoun, 421-461. Cambridge: The MIT Press, 1992.

Habermas, Jürgen. *Moral Consciousness and Communicative Action.* Translated by C. Lenhardt and S.W. Nicholsen. Cambridge MA: MIT Press, 1990.

Habermas, Jürgen. *Structural Transformation of the Public Sphere.* Cambridge, Mass: MIT Press, 1989.

Habermas, Jürgen. 'The Public Sphere: An Encyclopedia Article.' In *Critical Theory and Society: A Reader*, edited by Stephen Eric Bronner and Douglas Kellner, 136-142. New York: Routledge, 1989.

Habermas, Jürgen. *The Theory of Communicative Action,* Vol. I: *Reason and the Rationalization of Society.* Translated by Thomas McCarthy. London: Heinemann, 1984.

Habermas, Jürgen. *The Theory of Communicative Action,* Vol 2: *Lifeworld and System: A Critique of Functionalist Reason.* Translated by Thomas McCarthy. Boston: Beacon Press, 1987.

Habermas, Jürgen. *Toward a Rational Society: Student Protest, Science and Politics.* Translated by Jeremy Shapiro. Boston: Beacon Press, 1968.

Commentary:

Bohman, James, and William Rehg. 'Jürgen Habermas.' *The Stanford Encyclopedia of Philosophy* (Winter 2011 Edition), edited by Edward N. Zalta. http://plato.stanford.edu/archives/win2011/entries/habermas/.

Brand, Arie. *The Force of Reason: An Introduction to Habermas's Theory of Communicative Action.* Sydney: Allen and Unwin, 1990.

Finlayson, James Gordon. *Habermas: a Very Short Introduction.* New York: OUP, 2006.

Kellner, Douglas. 'Habermas, the Public Sphere, and Democracy: A Critical Intervention.' University of California, Los Angeles, Graduate School of Education and Information Studies, 2000. Accessed 20th March, 2013, http://pages.gseis.ucla.edu/faculty/kellner/essays/habermaspublicspheredemocracy.pdf.

Pusey, Michael. *Jürgen Habermas.* London: Routledge, 1988.

Practical Applications:

Ahearn, David Oki. 'Urban Empowerment as Public Participation: the Atlanta Project and Jürgen Habermas's Theory of Communicative Action.' *Annual of the Society of Christian Ethics* 20 (2000): 349-368.

Chilton, Stephen, and Maria Stalzer Wyant Cuzzo. 'Habermas's Theory of Communicative Action as a Theoretical Framework for Mediation Practice.' *Conflict Resolution Quarterly* 22, no. 3 (Spring 2005): 325-348.

Jacobson, Thomas L., and J. Douglas Storey. 'Development Communication and Participation: Applying Habermas to a Case Study of Population Programs in Nepal.' *Communication Theory* 14, no. 2 (May 2004): 99-121.

Kubacki, Steven R. 'Applying Habermas's Theory of Communicative Action to Values in Psychotherapy.' *Psychotherapy* 31 (Fall 1994): 463-477.

Seyyed Hossein Nasr

Biographical Introduction

Seyyed Hossein Nasr is a Muslim intellectual who was born in 1933 in Tehran, Iran. He is a professor at George Washington University, specialising in Islamic Studies. He is the author of over fifty books and five hundred articles[1] on topics including traditional metaphysics, Islamic science, religion and the environment, Sufism,[2] and Islamic philosophy. He also writes Sufi poetry, with a number of poetry collections to his name.[3]

In a number of his works, Nasr argues for and articulates a form of dialogue between religion and science. He is also very much concerned with interreligious dialogue and insists that 'for dialogue to happen, we need mutual understanding and empathy between religions.'[4] An important aspect of Nasr's dialogic discourse in this area is his view that it is their commonalities at the inner, spiritual level that makes meaningful dialogue possible between religions. This view is shaped by perennial philosophy, which had a profound effect on Nasr's thinking while he was a student of Frithjof Schuon. Perennial philosophy is the theory that the same profound truths can be discovered in a range of spiritual traditions because they have all been divinely revealed as legitimate spiritual paths. They contain truths from the same divine source.[5] Perennial philosophy is in evidence in Nasr's writings on philosophy, religion, spirituality, music, art, architecture, science, literature, civilisational dialogues, and the natural environment.

Nasr is deeply rooted in tradition, which he understands as 'the whole structure of thought that articulates the concepts embodied in the world of myth and symbols.'[6] He considers that tradition is alive, well and ripe for renewal. While Nasr criticises secularism and modernism for destroying the sense of the sacred in human societies, he does not advocate a regression to an idealised former era. Rather, he seeks to restore the sense of the sacred and the esoteric tradition (manifested as

---

1   A number of Nasr's articles can be found in the journal *Studies in Comparative Religion*.

2   Sufism is Islamic mysticism, sometimes referred to as the 'inner' dimension of Islam.

3   Seyyed Hossein Nasr, *Poems of the Way* (Oakton: Foundation for Traditional Studies, 1998).

4   Nasr and Jahanbegloo, *In Search of the Sacred: a Conversation with Seyyed Hossein Nasr on His Life and Thought* (California: ABC-CLIO, 2010), 290.

5   Terry Moore, introduction to *In Search of the Sacred*, by Nasr and Jahanbegloo, xxiv.

6   Terry Moore, introduction to *In Search of the Sacred*, xi.

Sufism in Islam) in the contemporary world.[7]

Nasr's serious engagement with other religions began early. At the age of twelve he left Iran for the United States and attended Peddie School in Hightstown, New Jersey, where all the students regularly attended church services. He recalls that he always felt able to appreciate and respect Christianity without developing any doubts about his own Islamic faith. Before moving to America he had, he says, 'a great love for Christ' as one of the prophets.[8] His career has involved theological dialogue not only with Christianity but also with Judaism, Hinduism, Buddhism and Confucianism. [9]

He is widely recognised for his work in comparative religion. He is also one of the few prominent Muslim intellectuals to be included as a volume in the Library of Living Philosophers, in the year 2000. He was also the first ever Muslim to give the Gifford lectures.

---

7   Terry Moore, introduction to *In Search of the Sacred*, xii.
8   Nasr and Jahanbegloo, *In Search of the Sacred,* 36.
9   Nasr and Jahanbegloo, *In Search of the Sacred*, 222.

Thought on Dialogue

Nasr's thought on dialogue can be approached from two different perspectives, as he proposes dialogue in two different spheres. In the first place, Nasr argues for dialogue between faith systems and their adherents.[10] His underlying understanding of religious diversity has its roots in perennial philosophy. He also explores the potential for constructive dialogue between religion and science.[11] He proposes that a sacred science can be re-discovered and developed by means of a process of respectful dialogue between religious truths and modern scientific discoveries.[12] Nasr offers an interesting perspective on dialogue in each of these two spheres; we will look at each in turn.

Underlying Nasr's approach to interreligious dialogue is his belief in the 'transcendent unity of all religions'. This idea is in accordance with perennial philosophy as set out by his teacher Frithjof Schuon. Nasr holds that all authentic religions are centred on 'a single Divine presence', and that this gives scope for adherents of all religions to find common ground.[13] At the outer level of theologies, religious forms, languages and so on, religions have significant differences. These differences are not to be erased or suppressed; they 'contribute to the plenitude of the garden of religion'.[14] At the same time, at the inner level, religions share profound mystical aspects which provide a natural basis for dialogue. The inner element that can allow for a dialogic engagement between religious faiths is what is called Sufism in Islam.[15]

The 'inner unity' among religions, propounded by such Muslim poets and mystics as Hafez, makes it possible for people of different faiths to engage in dialogue on a basis of real respect.[16] Thanks to the common ground shared by the two religions at the mystical level, Muslims can deeply respect Christianity and have great reverence for Jesus Christ as one of the Messengers of God, without in any way compromising their Islamic identity.[17] Such common ground is not restricted to the Abrahamic religions but provides scope for dialogue between monotheistic, polytheistic and even non-theistic traditions. Nasr argues that although polytheistic traditions

---

10   Seyyed Hossein Nasr, 'An Interview on Islam and Inter-religious Dialogue,' in *Universal Dimensions of Islam*, ed. Patrick Laude (World Wisdom, 2011).

11   Nasr, *The Essential Sophia* (World Wisdom, 2007), 210.

12   Nasr, *The Need for a Sacred Science* (SUNY Press, 1993), 166.

13   From this perspective, Nasr disputes the argument that the existence of different religions shows that none of them can be true in any absolute sense.

14   Nasr, 'An Interview on Islam and Inter-religious Dialogue,' 58.

15   Nasr, *Sufi Essays* (SUNY Press: New York, 1972), 32.

16   Nasr and Jahanbegloo, *In Search of the Sacred*, 35.

17   Nasr and Jahanbegloo, *In Search of the Sacred*, 35-36.

such as Hinduism maintain beliefs in a multitude of divinities, they still maintain the Unity doctrine that all beings have their source in one Supreme Being; they share this key notion with monotheists.[18] Nasr further notes that while clearly the Abrahamic traditions do not accept multiple divinities, a dialogic connection can be established between the names of God in the Islamic tradition and the various manifestations of one Supreme Being in polytheistic traditions such as Taoism (in its popular form) and the Hindu tradition.[19] Furthermore, Nasr holds that there is an *Urgrund* ('The Supreme Ground of Being') in both theistic traditions (such as Islam and Christianity) and non-theistic traditions (such as Buddhism and Confucianism) in the sense that all of these traditions hold that there is a Supreme Reality underlying all existence.[20]

In accordance with perennial philosophy that teaches that different religions share universal truths, Nasr argues that 'attitudes towards good and evil', attitudes 'towards nature, towards a vision of a spiritual reality that transcends the material, the possibility of spiritual wayfaring, spiritual realization, the sense of the sacred' and numerous other commonalities 'cut across the theological distinctions of monotheism, non-theism and polytheism.'[21] Nasr also emphasises that traditions across all these categories share common ground in their 'ethical and aesthetic teachings'.[22] Interreligious dialogue should focus on areas where there is some common ground. For instance, Christianity and Islam can enter into fruitful dialogue through the gates of metaphysics and theology, without jeopardising such constructive dialogue with political agendas.[23]

According to Nasr, dialogue, particularly interreligious dialogue, is a necessity. It serves a valuable purpose; by engaging in dialogue with each other, adherents of different religions 'gain deeper knowledge' about each other and grow in 'empathy for the other'.[24] It is also, he suggests, essential for the survival of religion into the future. Demanding a serious, responsible engagement with religious thought, dialogue is a safeguard against a general loss of interest in religion.

---

18   Nasr, 'An Interview on Islam and Inter-religious Dialogue,' 59.

19   Nasr, 'An Interview on Islam and Inter-religious Dialogue,' 59.

20   Nasr, 'An Interview on Islam and Inter-religious Dialogue,' 59.

21   Nasr, 'An Interview on Islam and Inter-religious Dialogue,' 59.

22   Nasr, 'An Interview on Islam and Inter-religious Dialogue,' 59.

23   Nasr, 'Islamic-Christian Dialogue: Problems and Obstacles to be Pondered and Overcome,' *The Muslim World*, 87, nos. 3-4 (July-October 1998): 218-237.

24   Nasr, 'An Interview on Islam and Inter-religious Dialogue,' 62.

Nasr stresses that interreligious dialogue does not mean losing one's own unique religious identity. He notes that those who engage in dialogue are often accused of betraying their faith, or of making compromises. He considers that if a person involved in dialogue remains faithful to the teachings of his tradition, there are no grounds for objection to his or her engagement. Indeed, interreligious dialogue is a religious duty.[25] However, Nasr does not consider this duty incumbent on every member of the Muslim community. He considers it on the level of *fardh kifayah*, meaning that while it is the duty of the religious community, it suffices if dialogue is put into practice by a segment of the religious community that has a proper understanding of what dialogue entails.[26] Individuals who have a good grounding in their own traditions and a good knowledge of other traditions provide a valuable service to their own community by engaging in dialogue. They can become 'a respected and trustworthy voice within their own community', facilitating healthy dialogue both with adherents of other religions and with their co-religionists not directly engaged in dialogue. The understanding of the 'other' they bring can lay the foundation of mutual respect and good relations between communities.[27]

Nasr emphasises that interreligious dialogue should not be confined to secular discussions at secular educational institutions. It is among religious people that dialogue will be carried out in a manner that maintains the essential sense of the sacred at the heart of religions and gives proper respect to their traditional formulations.[28]

Having considered the essential elements of Nasr's understanding of interreligious dialogue, we may now turn to his particular perspective on the possibility of dialogue between religion and science. Nasr's expertise both in the natural sciences and in theology places him in a promising position from which to broker a dialogue between these seemingly disparate areas. In our discussion of Nasr's thought on this area we will see three key principles for dialogue emerging. First, a balanced, dialogical relationship between different fields requires proper recognition of the distinct character of each. Second, power imbalances between the fields must be addressed before meaningful dialogue can be established. Thirdly, it takes considerable humility, thought and effort to prepare the ground for a fruitful dialogue between deeply divided fields.

Nasr is concerned to elucidate the scope, sources and methods of religion and of science; clarity on these issues is needed in order to ensure respect for the

---

25   Nasr, 'An Interview on Islam and Inter-religious Dialogue,' 60 f.

26   Nasr, 'An Interview on Islam and Inter-religious Dialogue,' 61.

27   Nasr, 'An Interview on Islam and Inter-religious Dialogue,' 63.

28   Nasr, 'An Interview on Islam and Inter-religious Dialogue,' 63.

essential nature of each field. Religion, and the authentic spirituality at its heart,[29] simultaneously treats reality as immanent and accepts it as transcendent, beyond categories and conceptualisations. Modern science,[30] on the other hand, views reality as something that can be measured by empirical analysis and verification, tending to assume that nothing exists outside the reach of empirical study.[31] This is by and large the perspective of modern science, although some scientists have differing personal views.[32] Science, without the aid of religious perspectives, inevitably 'absolutizes the relative',[33] treating matter and causalities as absolute reality and ignoring the real Absolute which is the concern of spirituality and of metaphysics, 'the science of the whole or of the totality'. While science and metaphysics observe and analyse different aspects of the same truth, it is metaphysics which offers access to the truth 'in its wholeness'.[34]

The current relationship between science and religion is not conducive to a healthy, mutually beneficial dialogue. In Nasr's words, 'dialogue is possible only among equals or those nearly equal.'[35] At the present time, science dominates perceptions of religion,[36] while modern interpretations of religion give in to this dominant position of modern science, sacrificing values and 'religious truths' in order to conform to changing scientific theories.[37] In the contemporary world science 'is almost deified and certainly absolutized, while its practitioners appear more and more to the masses at large as priests wielding ultimate authority over human life and even determining its meaning.'[38]

Because of the unbalanced relationship between religion and science, humankind has neglected the spiritual aspects of life, which are largely unchanged by time, and

---

29   Nasr notes that much confusion is introduced when people use the word 'spirituality' to mean anything from 'the inner, spiritual dimension of traditional religions' to a 'vague yearning for meaning' divorced from real religious experience or truth. He understands spirituality in the former sense. Nasr, *The Essential Sophia*, 209.

30   In the context of his discussion on the relationship between spirituality and science, Nasr defines science as 'that body of systematic knowledge of nature, combined with mathematics, which grew out of the Scientific Revolution of the 17th century on the basis of earlier Latin, Islamic and Greek sciences.' Nasr, *The Essential Sophia*, 208.

31   Nasr, *The Essential Sophia*, 210.

32   Nasr, *The Essential Sophia*, 210.

33   Nasr, *The Essential Sophia*, 210 f.

34   Nasr, *The Need for a Sacred Science*, 166.

35   Nasr, *The Need for a Sacred Science*, 166.

36   Nasr, *The Need for a Sacred Science*, 163.

37   Nasr, *The Essential Sophia*, 214, 216.

38   Nasr, *The Essential Sophia*, 207 f.

has abandoned tradition and the wisdom it contains.[39] The natural world is used without due consideration for its value and significance. Nasr argues that in light of the powerful influence of science in today's world and the ever present, even increasing yearning for spirituality in human beings, there is an urgent need for a better understanding between religion and science.[40]

The balance between the two areas needs to be redressed; science should not impose its rules and restrictions on religion or claim to be a '"source" for theology'.[41] Religious disciplines should have the right and the means to analyse and study the faculties of the mind and the works of nature, as much as philosophy and science.[42] They should do so through their *own* methods and sources, staying true to their own nature. Just as a scientist would not take theological methods into the laboratory, the theologian need have no recourse to the findings of the laboratory.[43]

In this context, Nasr designates the necessary steps towards understanding and dialogue between the principles and worldviews of science and religion. The first step is the recognition on the part of scientists that scientific theories, ever susceptible to change and correction with new discoveries and findings, will only ever offer understanding of a 'truncated version' of Reality, which is vast and unchanging.[44] This recognition may help to establish a 'shift of paradigm' and the possibility of recourse to the authentic spirituality of traditional religions.[45] This spiritual reality can give new meaning to modern science and its discoveries.

In this journey towards understanding and dialogue, a third step would be to define anew the meaning of spirituality in various religious traditions, and to identify its roots in divine revelation. There must be no ambiguity about the proper sources of authentic spirituality.[46] A further step would be for people knowledgeable in metaphysics to 'formulate a contemporary metaphysics of nature and cosmology', so that intellectual underpinnings for a new paradigm in modern science can be established.[47] Throughout these steps, religion should refrain from attempting to prove its spiritual realities through the lens of current scientific theories which, with

---

39   Nasr, *The Need for a Sacred Science*, 166.

40   Nasr, *The Essential Sophia*, 215.

41   Nasr, *The Need for a Sacred Science*, 163.

42   Nasr, *The Need for a Sacred Science*, 166.

43   Nasr, *The Need for a Sacred Science*, 166.

44   Nasr, *The Essential Sophia*, 215.

45   Nasr, *The Essential Sophia*, 216.

46   Nasr, *The Essential Sophia*, 216.

47   Nasr, *The Essential Sophia*, 216.

a new scientific breakthrough, may tomorrow become subject to amendment or change.[48] Through this series of developments a new paradigm of modern science could be established which would be at peace with religious truths, and cease to threaten nature and humankind with its 'exertion of power over the human psyche and the domain of nature'.[49]

The 'creation of a sacred science of the cosmos' is, Nasr considers, key to the process. This 'sacred science' would not annul the discoveries of modern science; rather, its function would be to offer a complementary kind of knowledge of the universe, a knowledge 'rooted in [the universe's] sacred reality'.[50] The knowledge it offered could 'discern between the aspects of modern science that correspond to some aspect of physical reality and those that are merely conjecture parading as science.'[51] By establishing a 'sacred view of nature' it would also prevent a ruthless exploitation of nature by humans.[52] Nasr notes that this type of approach, which harmonises spirituality with science, was known in traditional civilisations and can be observed in the scientific heritage of Muslim philosophers, such as works produced by Ibn Sina (Avicenna) and Ibn Rushd (Averroes).[53]

The establishment of a sacred science would have an ongoing dialogic function, creating a 'domain of discourse' bringing spirituality and science into dialogue with each other without demolishing the core realities of either.[54] For such a dialogic engagement to be possible considerable humility will be required. Modern science and the 'guardians and propagators of science' will need to give up a 'totalitarian and monopolistic view of science' and come to terms with other 'legitimate science[s] of nature' and with the limitations of their own approaches.[55] However, if there are sufficient efforts on the part of both religion and science the potential benefits to human society and the natural world are great. An understanding and ongoing dialogue between science and religion could help stall the ruthless exploitation of nature, and lead the way to a proper understanding of the 'metaphysical and symbolic significance of major modern scientific discoveries'.[56] Further, the 'void

---

48   Nasr, *The Essential Sophia*, 216.

49   Nasr, *The Essential Sophia*, 216.

50   Nasr, *The Essential Sophia*, 217.

51   Nasr, *The Essential Sophia*, 217.

52   Nasr, *The Essential Sophia*, 217.

53   Seyyed Hossein Nasr and Oliver Leaman, *History of Islamic Philosophy* (Routledge, 1997; 2002), 27.

54   Nasr, *The Essential Sophia*, 217.

55   Nasr, *The Essential Sophia*, 217.

56   Nasr, *The Essential Sophia*, 217.

and nihilism' that is experienced as a result of modernity may find an explanation and meaning through the perspective offered by religion.[57]

---

57   Nasr, *The Need for a Sacred Science*, 163.

Theory and Practice

The focus of this section will be on practice in interreligious dialogue, and especially on the advice Nasr offers on the practice of Christian-Muslim dialogue, based on his extensive experience in this particular area. Before we turn our attention to interreligious dialogue, though, it is worth noting that an interesting example of serious engagement between science and religion can be found in the Buddhist-science dialogues described in our chapter on the Dalai Lama. The 'Mind and Life' dialogues, in which the Dalai Lama has been engaged since 1987, are described by the Mind and Life Institute as 'a joint quest between scientists, philosophers and contemplatives to investigate the mind, develop a more complete understanding of the nature of reality, and promote well-being on the planet'.[58] Knowledgeable participants within each field allow the dialogues to draw seriously on the distinct sources of science and of religion. The dialogues have explored subjects including cosmology, ethics, altruism and education.[59]

Nasr has been a leading figure in dialogue not only with the other Abrahamic faiths but also with Hinduism and Buddhism. He has also sought to encourage dialogue between Islam and Confucianism.[60] His teaching at various universities across the United States and Iran has allowed him to share his ideas with numerous students, inspiring them too to explore dialogue between different religious and metaphysical traditions, and between science and spirituality. One of Nasr's students, Sachiko Murata, has made a great contribution to the understanding of an Islamic and Sufi metaphysics through the perspective of the metaphysical traditions of the Far East, such as Taoism, Buddhism and Confucianism.

Nasr's insight that the inner, spiritual aspect of religion is the best starting point for dialogue is mirrored in initiatives among various groups of spiritual practitioners. This approach is seen in the dialogues between Buddhist and Christian monks and nuns discussed in our chapter on the Dalai Lama. Another example is a series of dialogues between practitioners from the Sufi and Yogi traditions organised by the Global Peace Initiative of Women. The latest dialogue, entitled 'Sufi-Yogi Dialogue: The Nature of Oneness,' gathered fifteen leaders of respected spiritual traditions within Islam and Hinduism. The aim of the gathering was to achieve an in-depth understanding of the Ultimate Reality as represented in both traditions, and to explore the practical applications of this increased understanding towards

---

58   'Dialogues,' Mind and Life Institute, accessed 1ˢᵗ January, 2013, http://www.mindandlife. org/dialogues/.

59   'Dialogues.'

60   Nasr and Jahanbegloo, *In Search of the Sacred*, 222.

'meeting the critical global challenges facing us all today'.[61]

We will now briefly explore Nasr's insights on the particular obstacles to Islamic-Christian dialogue and the solutions he proposes for overcoming them. While critical of various aspects of the 'modern West' with which Christianity is so strongly associated, Nasr appreciates the inherent values of the religion itself and stresses the necessity of dialogue with its adherents despite the various difficulties involved.[62]

He contends that instead of focusing on key theological differences on the nature of God, Muslims and Christians should come together on the common ground of the monotheistic basis of both faiths, arguing that it is not hard to find the teaching of 'God as One' in both belief systems.[63] He states that where there are irreconcilable theological differences,

> The best that one can do... is to have respect for the other and for the Muslims at least to remember the Qur'anic verse, "and argue not with the People of the Scripture (including Christians) unless it be in a mostly kindly manner, save with such of them as do wrong; and say: We believe in that which hath been revealed unto us and revealed unto you; our God and your God is One, and unto Him we surrender"...The rest should be left in God's Hands.[64]

One particular contentious theological issue must be explored, he considers, or it will undermine the dialogue: the question of salvation. A fruitful dialogue cannot take place where some involved assume from the outset that the others are damned.

Other obstacles Nasr recognises relate to issues of how contemporary Christian and Muslim groups are treated by each other in different countries. He discusses freedom of worship and missionary activity. Nasr postulates that it is important to 'bring out clearly the principles as well as the facts involved' and discuss the issues with honesty and fairness.[65] He further argues that it is important to respect the right of other religious communities to different forms of religious expression, and not to demand exact reciprocity in all matters. For example, Christians cannot claim a right to visit Mecca on the basis that Muslims may visit the Vatican; the way in which the two faiths honour their most sacred sites are different, but both are legitimate.

---

61   'Report on Sufi-Yogi Dialogue,' Seven Pillars House, accessed 1st January, 2013, http://www.sevenpillarshouse.org/article/report_on_sufi-yogi_dialogue/.

62   Nasr and Jahanbegloo, *In Search of the Sacred*, xxiii-xxiv.

63   Nasr, 'Islamic-Christian Dialogue,' 218-237.

64   Nasr, 'Islamic-Christian Dialogue,' 220 f. The Qur'anic reference is to the Holy Qur'an, trans. Pickthall, 29:46.

65   Nasr, 'Islamic-Christian Dialogue,' 225, 231.

A further obstacle to dialogue that Nasr identifies is opposition from exclusivist groups who fear that dialogue will undermine their religious identity. Persistent engagement in dialogue by devout believers of good standing in their own religious community can help gradually to dispel this fear; it demonstrates to co-religionists that those engaged in dialogue do not become less religious or less pious by being involved in it.[66] Courage is required, and a steadfast devotion to one's own religion. In face of the suspicion of some sceptical Muslims that dialogue is a Christian initiative, Nasr points out that historically, Muslim societies have often been in dialogue with the adherents of other religions, giving the examples of the Ottoman State and Andalusian Spain.[67]

Nasr also discusses the troublesome interference of modernism as an unacknowledged third party in dialogue. He argues that Muslim groups engaged in dialogue, who are not themselves religiously affected by modernism, may mistakenly believe that they are talking with Christians whose faith is the same as that of early Christian theologians, which may cause confusion. As such, Nasr holds that it should be made clear whether the religious outlook of the groups involved in dialogue has been affected by modernism.[68] As in Nasr's discussion of science and religion, clarity in dialogue is a pervasive concern here.

Nasr hopes that while obstacles to Islamic-Christian dialogue are significant, 'with good will, love for truth and charity rather than passion, fanaticism and love for power, most of these obstacles can be overcome.'[69] The same attitude of realism combined with hope shines through his comments on the relationship between science and religion. Not everyone will be able or willing to engage fruitfully in dialogue in either context and Nasr does not see *universal* engagement in dialogue as a necessity or a religious requirement. Yet in both of the contexts discussed here the stakes are high and the potential benefits of dialogue are immense.

---

66   Nasr, 'An Interview on Islam and Inter-religious Dialogue,' 62.

67   Nasr, 'An Interview on Islam and Inter-religious Dialogue,' 63.

68   Nasr, 'Islamic-Christian Dialogue: Problems and Obstacles to be Pondered and Overcome,' *The Muslim World,* 87, nos. 3-4 (July-October 1998): 232 ff.

69   Nasr, 'Islamic-Christian Dialogue', 236.

Questions for Reflection

1. Is interreligious dialogue between select representatives of each religious community sufficient for interreligious understanding?

2. Nasr considers that there must be clarity about whether a religious group involved in dialogue has or has not been affected by the influence of modernism. How, in practice, could this be achieved?

3. Is any kind of dialogue possible between people who consider each other to be excluded from salvation?

4. What benefits do you consider might follow from the kind of religion-science relationship proposed by Nasr?

5. Do you agree with Nasr's statement that 'dialogue is possible only among equals or those nearly equal'?[70] What level of power imbalance, if any, is compatible with dialogue?

6. Nasr states that a sacred science of the cosmos could 'discern between the aspects of modern science that correspond to some aspect of physical reality and those that are merely conjecture parading as science.'[71]

   a. Nasr is adamant that science cannot be a source for religion. But does he consider that religion might be a valid source for science?

   b. Is the relationship that Nasr envisages between science and religion a dialogical relationship? Are science and religion 'equals or nearly equal' in his eyes?

---

70   Nasr, *The Need for a Sacred Science*, 166.
71   Nasr, *The Essential Sophia*, 217.

Bibliography

Mind and Life Institute. 'Dialogues.' Accessed 25th December, 2012. http://www.mindandlife.org/dialogues/.

Nasr, Seyyed Hossein. 'An Interview on Islam and Inter-religious Dialogue.' In *Universal Dimensions of Islam*, edited by Patrick Laude, 57-65. Indiana: World Wisdom, 2011.

Nasr, Seyyed Hossein. *History of Islamic Philosophy: Part I*. Routledge: London, 1997, 2002.

Nasr, Seyyed Hossein. *Islam: Religion, History, and Civilization*. San Francisco: Harper Collins, 2010.

Nasr, Seyyed Hossein. 'Islamic-Christian Dialogue: Problems and Obstacles to be Pondered and Overcome.' *The Muslim World*, 87, nos. 3-4 (July-October 1998): 218-237.

Nasr, Seyyed Hossein. *Poems of the Way*. Oakton: Foundation for Traditional Studies, 1999.

Nasr, Seyyed Hossein. 'Spirituality and Science: Convergence or Divergence?' In *The Essential Sophia*, 207-218. Canada: World Wisdom, 2007.

Nasr, Seyyed Hossein. *Sufi Essays*. SUNY Press: New York, 1972.

Nasr, Seyyed Hossein. *The Essential Seyyed Hossein Nasr*. Edited by William Chittick. Canada: World Wisdom, 2007.

Nasr, Seyyed Hossein. *The Need for a Sacred Science*. New York: State University of New York Press, 1993.

Nasr, Seyyed Hossein and Ramin Jahanbegloo. *In Search of the Sacred: a Conversation with Seyyed Hossein Nasr on His Life and Thought*. California: ABC-CLIO, 2010.

Seven Pillars House. 'Report on Sufi-Yogi Dialogue.' Accessed 1st March, 2013. http://www.sevenpillarshouse.org/article/report_on_sufi-yogi_dialogue/.

Recommended Reading

Nasr's Works:

Nasr, Seyyed Hossein. 'An Interview on Islam and Inter-religious Dialogue.' In *Universal Dimensions of Islam*, edited by Patrick Laude, 57-65. Indiana: World Wisdom, 2011.

Nasr, Seyyed Hossein. *Islam: Religion, History, and Civilization*. San Francisco: Harper Collins, 2010.

Nasr, Seyyed Hossein. 'Islamic-Christian Dialogue: Problems and Obstacles to be Pondered and Overcome.' *The Muslim World*, 87, nos. 3-4 (July-October 1998): 218-237.

Nasr, Seyyed Hossein. Spirituality and Science: Convergence or Divergence? In *The Essential Sophia*, 207-218. Canada: World Wisdom, 2007.

Nasr, Seyyed Hossein. *Sufi Essays*. SUNY Press: New York, 1972.

Nasr, Seyyed Hossein. *The Need for a Sacred Science*. New York: State University of New York Press, 1993.

Commentary:

Nasr, Seyyed Hossein, Randall E. Auxier, and Lucian W. Stone. *The Philosophy of Seyyed Hossein Nasr*. Chicago: Open Court, 2001.

Nasr, Seyyed Hossein, and William C. Chittick. *The Essential Seyyed Hossein Nasr*. Bloomington, Ind: World Wisdom, 2007.

Nasr, Seyyed Hossein and Ramin Jahanbegloo. *In Search of the Sacred: a Conversation with Seyyed Hossein Nasr on His Life and Thought*. California: ABC-CLIO, 2010.

Practical Applications:

Nasr, Seyyed Hossein. 'Islamic-Christian Dialogue: Problems and Obstacles to be Pondered and Overcome.' *The Muslim World*, 87, nos. 3-4 (July-October 1998): 218-237.

Maura O'Neill

Biographical Introduction

Maura O'Neill is the author of two books exploring the current and potential future role of women in interreligious dialogue, and the challenges they face. She is Professor Emerita at Chaffey College in Rancho Cucamonga, California, where she taught philosophy and religious studies as Professor of Philosophy for twenty-one years. She also served as advisor to the Muslim Student Association. Since her retirement in 2007 she has continued to pursue her research and her longstanding engagement in dialogue with women of different faiths.

O'Neill was born in New York. She started her career as a nun in a Roman Catholic religious order. She reports that it was while living in the convent that she became a feminist. She was impressed by the scholarship of the sisters she lived with, and their independence from men.[1] She graduated from Brentwood College, New York and later received an M.A. in Theology from St Michael's College, Vermont. She worked as a teacher in schools in Puerto Rico as well as in the United States.

She left the religious order after fifteen years and took up a post as Catholic Campus Minister at Cal State San Bernardino and San Bernardino Valley College. While in this post she completed her doctorate in philosophy of religion and theology at Claremont Graduate University.

O'Neill's two books on women in interreligious dialogue draw on her personal experiences in dialogue with women of different faiths, as well as on diverse reports and reflections from other academics and practitioners. Her experience underlies her sense of the inadequacy of dialogue that sidelines women and her insistence on the need for women to engage in dialogue among themselves. Personal experience also grounds her understanding of the great range and complexity of identities represented in women's interreligious dialogue, and of the transformation of perspectives that can occur when individuals are allowed to explain their own perspectives in their own words. Her appreciation of the diversity of ways in which women conceive of freedom and oppression began with hearing the perspective of an American convert to Islam who wore a headscarf: 'She said that the American

---

1   'Lecturer Challenges Religious Stereotypes,' Muslim Heretics Conference, accessed 19ᵗʰ May, 2012, http://tabari.com/blog1/2009/04/05/lecturer-challenges-religious-stereotypes-inland-news-pecom-southern-california-news-news-for-inland-southern-california/.

feminist movement was necessary because American women suffered far more oppression than Muslim women did. I was amazed...' [2] In the preface of her second book, which explores the challenge of bringing progressive and conservative perspectives *within* religions into dialogue, she mentions a personal impetus for the project. The book is, in part, an attempt to 'understand, grapple with and reweave' her relationship with a dear friend from a different Christian tradition, after a series of painful arguments about religion and politics.[3]

In both her books O'Neill highlights the case for interreligious dialogue among women. However, her work can inform practitioners of all kinds of dialogue. It includes strategies for dialogue and valuable insights on its complexities, its potential, and its relation to social action.

---

2   Maura O'Neill, *Mending a Torn World: Women in Interreligious Dialogue* (New York: Orbis Books, 2007), 17.

3   O'Neill, *Mending a Torn World,* ix f.

Thought on Dialogue

Maura O'Neill's contribution to dialogue theory is in the area of interreligious dialogue, which she defines as 'persons communicating about their relationship with and experience of the ultimate reality or realities.'[4] She considers that since religion shapes individual and group identities, dialogue at the religious level is crucial for the formation of respectful, resilient relationships between people of different religious positions. It is becoming increasingly important in a world in which the political and ideological conflicts which polarise societies are often framed in religious terms. At its best, O'Neill considers that interreligious dialogue can 'break down barriers, dissolve animosities, and build bridges to a future of understanding and peace.'[5]

Thus far, though, interreligious dialogue has not been inclusive enough to achieve its full potential. It has suffered from two key deficiencies. Firstly, women and their concerns have been vastly underrepresented in the dialogue. Dialogue has been one-sided, sidelining the distinctive experience and insights of women.[6] Secondly, interreligious dialogue has left out the conservative elements of religious traditions, undermining the peace-making potential of the process by leaving too many groups, including fundamentalist groups, outside the conversation. O'Neill defines 'conservatives' in the religious context as those who feel that their religious tradition needs to be protected against the changes brought about by modern research and social developments. Progressives are those who look favourably on most of these changes and apply findings of modern research to the interpretation of religious experience. Major differences in experience and perspectives make it clear that progressives cannot presume to speak for conservatives in dialogue, nor men for women.

The lack of involvement of religious conservatives in interreligious dialogue can be accounted for by entrenched prejudices between conservatives and progressives within religious traditions. While conservative groups often see progressives as compromising their religious principles, progressives suspect that conservatives will subvert dialogue by trying to convert others.[7]

---

4   Maura O'Neill, *Women Speaking, Women Listening: Women in Interreligious Dialogue* (New York: Orbis Books, 1990), 3.

5   O'Neill, *Mending a Torn World*, 125.

6   O'Neill notes that 'modern psychological and philosophical studies reveal that gender is an important factor in the way religions are lived and experienced.' *Mending a Torn World*, 5.

7   O'Neill, *Mending a Torn World*, 5, 103.

O'Neill's exploration of the factors excluding women from dialogue demonstrates how pervasive and subtle the barriers to inclusive dialogue can be.[8] She explains that the philosophical concepts involved in the very definition of 'interreligious dialogue' are profoundly marked by a history of male dominance. Philosophical notions of what a person is, of how knowledge is acquired, and of what human qualities are most valuable are biased towards the men who developed them. In addition, in religions such as Judaism and Christianity, the persistent use of male imagery such as 'father' and 'king' for God has subtly encouraged a view of men alone as God's true heirs and representatives. In the realm of communication, the more personal kinds of speech associated with women and their roles have been devalued in relation to public, male genres. However, when women respond by mastering male speech genres, they are not properly attended to because men are unreceptive to hearing women speak in this context. Across the spectrum of intellectual and social practices, women have been marginalised. Contemporary male theologians who speak about 'man' or 'persons' may imagine that they are speaking of and for men and women, but in reality they are concerned with the male half of the species which has been focused on and favoured by the intellectual world for so many centuries.

O'Neill proposes that in order to address the profoundly male-dominated nature of dialogue it is not enough simply to invite more women to interreligious meetings; sometimes genuine inclusion requires more creative strategies than simply extending the guest list. Women need to engage in dialogue among themselves. O'Neill explains, 'Only then will they have the assurance of being heard, and, because their language and style of communication is understood, real dialogue can take place.'[9] In the course of that dialogue women will be able to clarify their own and each other's identities, and to establish the issues that they wish to bring to mixed dialogue. It is worth underlining that O'Neill considers women's dialogue to be a step towards achieving a genuinely inclusive dialogue, not simply an end in itself.[10]

Through dialogue among themselves women can come to a mature understanding not only of each other's religious identities, but of the forms of oppression with which different women struggle. Sometimes this process is painful. O'Neill describes how hearing of the experiences of other women who longed to be priests heightened her sense of the injustice of her own exclusion from this role. When, following these conversations, she attended an ordination, the injustice of this exclusion hit

8   O'Neill, *Women Speaking, Women Listening*, 3-50.

9   O'Neill, *Women Speaking, Women Listening*, 49.

10   O'Neill, *Women Speaking, Women Listening*, x.

her and a joyous occasion became, for her, one of 'extreme pain'.[11] Hearing about others' experiences of oppression can distressingly highlight one's own. A woman in dialogue might also have the difficult experience of finding that she has herself been involved in the oppression or exclusion of a group represented in the dialogue.[12]

Oppression is a theme that commonly surfaces in women's dialogue. Efforts to secure full respect for women and end their oppression are a global phenomenon.[13] However, different women have very different notions of what constitutes 'respect' and 'oppression'. A North American woman might see veiling as evidence of male oppression while an Egyptian woman considers it an empowering rejection of superficiality and male exploitation.[14] Western feminists have sometimes been guilty of an imperialistic approach, telling other women what kind of freedom they should want. Further, women within any given religion understand the relationship of their tradition to their own dignity and wellbeing in a range of different ways. For instance, Christianity encompasses women who feel fulfilled in living according to Biblical gender roles, and women who believe that the Bible reflects the oppressive patriarchy of its time and who find liberation in a radical reinterpretation of Christian scripture and theology.[15] These variations present a real challenge for mutual understanding. However, through exploring one another's experiences in dialogue women can work towards a fuller understanding of the needs and aspirations of others and themselves.

O'Neill emphasises that dialogue's exploration of oppression and liberation is not a way of avoiding action on injustice, or of explaining it away by saying that it is all culturally relative. 'Rather,' she writes, 'it is an honest endeavour that seeks to discover, through conversation, the reality of oppression and to separate that reality from what is truly culturally relative.'[16] Such painstaking reflection on oppression, in women's dialogue and in dialogue with any marginalised groups, can prepare the way for properly considered and wise social action where action is needed.

The importance of women's dialogue stems not only from the requirements of fairness and the benefits of exploring oppression through dialogue, but also from the world's real need of women's insights and skills. Women's voices, issuing from their distinctive life experiences, can revitalise and rebalance dialogue by introducing

---

11   O'Neill, *Women Speaking, Women Listening*, 101.

12   O'Neill describes such an experience in *Women Speaking, Women Listening*, 102.

13   O'Neill, *Women Speaking, Women Listening*, 59

14   O'Neill, *Women Speaking, Women Listening*, 58.

15   O'Neill, *Mending a Torn World*, 25 ff.

16   O'Neill, *Women Speaking, Women Listening*, 104.

fresh perspectives on the meaning, purpose and processes of dialogue.[17] Further, O'Neill suggests that, for whatever combination of reasons of biology and social conditioning, 'expressing emotions and communicating on a personal level are more commonly seen in women than in men.' These abilities are valuable resources for dialogue.[18]

Partly for this reason, O'Neill suggests that women's dialogue is the best starting point for the difficult but vital work of intrafaith dialogue which brings progressives and conservatives from a particular religion together. An additional reason for kick-starting this work among women is that women's issues are frequently at the heart of disagreements between religious conservatives and progressives.[19] O'Neill's hope is that 'if women's dialogue can help increase mutual understanding, and if women then achieve a greater voice in the larger forum, such understanding might spread, thus laying the foundation for a more trusting environment in which peace becomes a possibility.'[20]

Several obstacles make it difficult for different groups within a religion to come together. These need to be understood and addressed. One of these obstacles is stereotyping. Conservatives will often stereotype progressives as self-centred and quick to abandon religious principles, while progressives frequently see conservatives as 'narrow-minded, insecure, and out of touch with the real world and global problems.'[21] The problem is exacerbated by the selective information that each group accesses about the other. In an increasingly polarised world, people tend to associate with people with similar views and subscribe to the media that support those views. Their one-sided views thus go unchallenged.

A third obstacle to be overcome is the fear of loss of identity. Since religion constitutes such an integral part of many people's identities, they often feel anxious

---

17   See O'Neill, *Women Speaking, Women Listening*, 3-49. O'Neill notes the more holistic ideas of the human person, knowledge and ethics which issue from contemporary women's thought. Feminist thinkers are among those challenging the sharp dichotomies (reason and culture, reason and nature, reason and intuition, and absolutism and relativism) that male thinkers have historically taken for granted. Such approaches can shed helpful new light on the process of dialogue. Holistic views of the person, as essentially embodied as well as rational, encourage the fruitful inclusion of the personal along with the theological in dialogue. O'Neill also explains how the feminist writer Anne Seller hints at a helpful epistemology (theory of knowledge) in which knowledge is tested and developed through the process of conversation (*Women Speaking, Women Listening*, 18 ff).

18   O'Neill, *Mending a Torn World*, 7.

19   O'Neill, *Mending a Torn World*, 6.

20   O'Neill, *Mending a Torn World*, xv.

21   O'Neill, *Mending a Torn World*, 103.

about exposing themselves to people who may question their beliefs. This anxiety can lead to defensiveness and ultimately conflict. Each of these obstacles to coming together is intensified where the encounter is between people of different positions within the same faith. O'Neill explains, 'We think that they should share our beliefs because we claim we share the same tradition.' Accordingly, when confronted with real differences, 'we tend to blame the other for veering off the straight path.'[22]

Careful attention to the methodology of dialogue can help dialogue facilitators to navigate these challenges. O'Neill proposes several methods for women's dialogue, applicable to intrafaith as well as interfaith situations.[23] They are also well worth the consideration of dialogue facilitators working outside the areas of religious dialogue or women's dialogue. First, it is vital that the purpose of coming together is made clear. O'Neill notes that, 'In order for there to be a sincere exchange of ideas and experiences, trust is essential, and the biggest obstacle to trust is a hidden agenda.'[24] If participants come together expecting dialogue and find that others are trying to engage them in debate and change their minds, trust is completely undermined. In intrafaith dialogue there is a particular temptation to try and argue the other round to the 'correct' position. Therefore, clarity about the purpose of the meeting is particularly important.

It is also important for facilitators to find constructive ways of using conflict. O'Neill notes that conflict is inevitable in women's dialogue, and anger is a frequent feature, perhaps because such dialogue provides a rare forum in which women's anger can be expressed and heard. Conflict must be well managed if trust is to be maintained, but it may be a source of growth and insight. Conflict highlights genuine disagreements which can then be explored and perhaps resolved, rather than being dismissed only to resurface in a more destructive form. Thoughtful facilitation can ensure that issues likely to bring conflict are explored in a helpful way. In women's dialogue, conflict often develops over different experiences and understandings of oppression in relation to religion. This thorny area may be productively broached through a session in which each person is invited to explain positive and negative elements of her experience of religion. Such a structure gives each participant space to express herself on a contentious issue and enhances mutual understanding.[25]

---

22   O'Neill, *Mending a Torn World*, 104 f.

23   The three strategies discussed by O'Neill in *Mending a Torn World* are, she notes, drawn from the methods mentioned in 'Fostering Dialogue Across Divides,' a workbook published by the North American non-profit dialogue organisation the Public Conversations Project, http://www.publicconversations.org/ (accessed 19th May, 2012). See *Mending a Torn World*, 106.

24   O'Neill, *Mending a Torn World*, 109.

25   O'Neill, *Women Speaking, Women Listening*, 94 ff.

Active listening is another key element of dialogue. Real listening is a skill that requires effort and practice. O'Neill refers to the work of Kay Lindahl, director of the Listening Center, Los Angeles. Lindahl's workshops emphasise the need to prepare oneself to listen, and the value of asking for points of clarification.[26]

A final technique advocated by O'Neill is the use of personal story.[27] Personal stories can establish an atmosphere of trust; it is easier to trust people when we know their stories. Establishing trust is crucial for women to find the confidence to speak for themselves; the long history of the marginalisation of women's voices has left a legacy of reticence. Personal story also prevents dialogue from becoming too abstract and disconnected from the participants' lives.

In addition, it clarifies the diverse perspectives of participants and sheds light on points of commonality and distinction. By listening to each other's stories, participants avoid making premature assumptions and start to gain a real appreciation of diversity. When differences surface in the context of personal story they are less likely to have a divisive effect. Stories naturally draw people into the perspective of the teller. Even if the hearer disagrees strongly with the teller's position, she will often find new respect for the sincerity of that position and come to appreciate its basis in the storyteller's own experience.[28] Accordingly, personal story is an invaluable method for exploring challenging but important topics, such as sexuality and gender roles and the nature of religious authority.[29]

O'Neill's work expresses the aspiration that earnest efforts in women's interfaith and intrafaith dialogue will pave the way for truly inclusive dialogue embracing men and women, conservatives and progressives. She has high hopes for what can be achieved by genuinely inclusive dialogue. In dialogue which truly attends to the voices of women as well as men, 'new truths will be discovered that are beyond those already known: truths about men and about women, about their relationship to one another and to God.'[30] When progressives and conservatives can overcome the obstacles to dialogue they will, through hearing each other's stories, learn to respect and value one another and to work together for justice and peace.[31] Extraordinary things are possible if we have 'the courage to acknowledge our finitude, the love to embrace the other's differences, and the perseverance to settle for nothing less than a renewed face of the earth.'[32]

---

26   O'Neill, *Mending a Torn World*, 112 f.

27   O'Neill, *Women Speaking, Women Listening*, 89 ff.

28   O'Neill, *Mending a Torn World*, 45.

29   O'Neill, *Mending a Torn World*, 114 ff.

30   O'Neill, *Women Speaking, Women Listening*, 106.

31   O'Neill, *Mending a Torn World*, 128.

32   O'Neill, *Women Speaking, Women Listening*, 106.

Theory and Practice

O'Neill's perspective on dialogue is shaped by extensive engagement in dialogue. Her books argue for a particular practice, women's dialogue, as well as offering strategies for this dialogue. Her insights, both on the unique characteristics and potential of women's dialogue, and on promising dialogue methods, are supported by a range of other practitioners.

A number of women reflecting on the women's dialogue which O'Neill considers so important share her appreciation of the quality of listening in women-only groups which allows women to find their voices. Sevgi Basman, who has organised women's events at the Dialogue Society's Manchester Branch, reports that they 'help women to communicate more as there may be some women who are shy when it is a mixed environment.'

Ruth Tetlow, an interfaith dialogue practitioner who has conducted research with women in dialogue in Birmingham, also observes that women frequently value women-only environments for the 'listening space' they provide. They can be particularly helpful to 'women from cultures where women and men traditionally live separate lives [including south and east Asian cultures].'[33] The liberating effect of the women-only environment is seen in the popular Birmingham Women's Peace Group, a diverse group of women meeting monthly to explore identities and look at possibilities for social action.[34] Tetlow, like O'Neill, also notes the importance of story in women's dialogue, remarking that personal story 'avoids the pitfall of making unfounded generalizations... and helps to ground the discussion in lived reality.'[35]

Tetlow also agrees that women's dialogue makes a distinctive, potentially transformative contribution to interfaith dialogue. Women introduce a more holistic approach to dialogue, bringing together the personal and the intellectual.[36]

---

33 Ruth Tetlow, 'The Missing Dimension: Women and Inter Faith Encounter in Birmingham,' *Current Dialogue* 46 (2005).

34 Tetlow, 'The Missing Dimension.' See also 'Your Community: Sharing love between our city's faiths,' Birmingham Mail, 2nd November, 2010, accessed 21st May, 2012, http:// www.birminghammail.net/news/your-news/2010/11/02/your-community-sharing-love-between-our-city-s-faiths-97319-27585594/.

35 Tetlow, 'The Missing Dimension.'

36 Tetlow cites the following reflection from a woman in her research group: 'Maybe encounter is a better word (than dialogue) because dialogue tends to suggest that it's what you do with your mouths and it goes into your ears, whereas what we're talking about is using our hearts, our eyes and our senses, out intuition, our instinct and also the things that are beyond putting into words. When we step into the area of our faith lives, our spiritual lives, there's a whole lot you can't say, but we try to hear that... And sense it from each other ...' Tetlow, 'The Missing Dimension.'

Women's dialogue highlights the need to reconsider a range of theological categories. Finally, women's initiatives, such as the Birmingham Women's Peace Group, display a particular concern with peace and justice. O'Neill, who also notes this feature, commends this concern but warns women not to focus on shared action to the neglect of deeper interreligious dialogue; resilient cooperative relationships demand real mutual understanding.[37]

Galia Golan and Zahira Kamal have also noted distinct advantages to women's dialogue in the context of peace-building dialogue in Palestine and Israel. Here, women have tended to outnumber men in grass roots dialogue, although they are underrepresented at more official levels. Golan and Kamal note the value of women's readiness for personal engagement, their focus on humanitarian concerns and their strong identification with the grass roots as opposed to elites. Such features of women's dialogue can be effective in 'dismantl[ing] the dehumanisation and demonization of the enemy.'[38] Women's dialogue also has certain distinctive weaknesses; women are sometimes unwilling to tackle difficult issues, which consequently remain unresolved. Nevertheless, Golan and Kamal suggest, efforts at conflict transformation in Palestine and Israel would considerably benefit from the expansion of women's influences.

Women's engagement with the grass roots and their personal approach to dialogue are also noted in Kathryn Lohre's survey of the growing numbers of women's dialogue initiatives in America since 9/11. She writes:

> women's interfaith initiatives offer an exciting alternative to the standard model for interfaith engagement...academic and professional authorities on interfaith relations are replaced with real-life experts: women who live and breathe the challenges of religious coexistence in times of crisis. ...formal dialogue is replaced with storytelling.[39]

Lohre introduces a wide range of dialogue projects, noting several common features. Initiatives often begin with a personal invitation from one woman to another, as in the case of Women Transcending Boundaries, a popular interfaith group founded after a woman from a church in Syracuse sought contact with Muslim women in her community. Storytelling, and a social element to proceedings are also common features of women's interfaith activities.

---

37   O'Neill, *Mending a Torn World,* 100.

38   Galia Golan and Zahira Kamal, 'Women's People-to-People Activities: Do We Do It Better?' *Palestine-Israel Journal of Politics, Economics and Culture* 12/13, no. 4/1 (2005), Available at: http://www.pij.org/details.php?id=403.

39   Kathryn Lohre, 'Women's Interfaith Initiatives in the United States Post 9/11,' *Interreligious Insight* 5, no. 2 (2007).

It seems that, in whatever context it occurs, women's dialogue is characterised by features and insights that have a lot to offer the wider world of dialogue. The growth of such dialogue which Lohre notes in North America is a step towards the truly inclusive mixed dialogue which O'Neill sees as the ultimate goal.

O'Neill's recognition of the importance of intrafaith dialogue, and of the need to include conservative groups as well as progressives in dialogue, is shared by other dialogue practitioners. Professor Ian Linden of the Tony Blair Faith Foundation, speaking at the Dialogue Society's 'Making Dialogue Effective' discussion series, noted that intrafaith dialogue with hard-line groups within any religion is often more challenging than interfaith dialogue.[40] However, sidelining such groups can create further discord by making them feel betrayed by their community. Several other contributors expressed similar opinions.

While there is undoubtedly room for further efforts in this difficult but crucial area of dialogue, some groups have already taken up the challenge. O'Neill gives the example of the Buddhist women's groups Sakyadhita, which brings together women from different Buddhist traditions and perspectives to build mutual understanding and reflect together on the future of women in Buddhism.[41]

Within the Christian tradition in the UK, 'Churches Together' works at the 'four nations', national, and local level to build relationships between different Christian denominations.[42] It is worth noting, also, instances in which representatives of the conservative, evangelical end of the Christian spectrum, which is not generally associated with dialogue, have taken active steps towards interfaith engagement. In 2010 St Ethelburga's Centre for Reconciliation and Peace, in London, hosted sixty evangelical Christians for a consultation exploring issues around interfaith encounter.[43] One participant and speaker, Dr Andrew Smith, has been arranging youth activities bringing Christians and Muslims together since 2000.[44]

---

40   Dialogue Society, *Making Dialogue Effective*, (London: Dialogue Society, 2013), 31 f. Available on the Dialogue Society website, http://www.dialoguesociety.org/publications/Making-Dialogue-Effective.pdf.

41   O'Neill, *Mending a Torn World*, 95, 101.

42   Churches Together, accessed 22nd May, 2012, http://www.churches-together.net/Groups/42314/Churches_Together_in.aspx.

43   'Evangelicals explore interfaith encounter at St Ethelburga's,' St Ethelburga's Centre for Reconciliation and Peace, accessed 22nd May, 2012, http://stethelburgas.org/evangelicals-explore-interfaith-encounter-st-ethelburgas.

44   These projects were initially carried out within his work with the Scripture Union and then with The Feast, a charity which he founded in 2008: http://www.thefeast.org.uk/about/history/ (accessed 20th May, 2012).

The Corrymeela Community in Ireland has been a pioneer of particularly difficult intrafaith dialogue, bringing together Catholics and Protestants separated by political and religious differences coloured by long years of division and conflict.

The work of this ecumenical, peace-building community illustrates the effectiveness of one of the strategies for dialogue advocated by O'Neill: storytelling. Justine Darling explains that 'the telling of stories helped humanize individuals from opposing groups by emphasizing basic human emotions of sadness, loss, and fear.'[45] The trust created through exchange of personal stories provided a foundation for further community development projects. Personal story is also a key tool used by St Ethelburga's Centre, which has developed a helpful guide to the use of story.[46]

One of the other key dialogue strategies mentioned by O'Neill, active listening, is exemplified in the practice of Kay Lindahl of the Listening Centre, as mentioned in the previous section. The importance of active listening is also underlined by Daniel Yankelovich, who identifies 'listening with empathy' as one of the essential conditions for dialogue. The organisations he has founded and worked with, which are discussed in this volume's chapter on Yankelovich, seek to design and facilitate dialogues in which people are able to listen actively.

Again, the importance of clarifying the purpose of dialogue is recognised by other practitioners along with O'Neill. Speaking at the Dialogue Society, conflict transformation experts Dr Diana Francis and Dr Marwan Darweish underlined the importance of establishing an agreed purpose so that the dialogue proceeds with the informed consent of all involved.[47] All the strategies mentioned in this section are also stressed by non-profit dialogue organisation the Public Conversation Project in a resource cited by O'Neill.[48]

The dialogue strategies commended by O'Neill, and her other insights, can be and indeed are helpfully applied to diverse dialogue situations in women's groups and mixed groups.

---

45   Justine Darling, *Restorative Justice: A Tool in Rebuilding Post-Conflict Northern Ireland,* DigitalCollections@SIT, 2012. http://digitalcollections.sit.edu/conflict_reconcilation_symposium/jan11/memoryhealingpanel/3/.

46   'What's your story?' St Ethelburga's Centre for Reconciliation and Peace, accessed 22nd May, 2012. Available at: http://stethelburgas.org/narrative-resource.

47   Dialogue Society, *Making Dialogue Effective,* 17.

48   See 'Fostering Dialogue Across Divides,' Public Conversations Project, accessed 22nd May, 2012, http://www.publicconversations.org/docs/resources/Jams_website.pdf. The Public Conversation Project facilitates dialogue on a range of contentious social issues as well as providing training and resources for dialogue.

Questions for Reflection

1. O'Neill sees women's dialogue as a stepping stone to a more inclusive mixed dialogue.

    a. Will it work?

    b. Are there any potential pitfalls in her approach?

    c. At what stage, if any, would women's (only) dialogue become unnecessary?

2. Do you feel you interact with people differently in a single-sex dialogue context? In what way? In your experience, is the dialogue more or less sincere/relaxed/meaningful/profound in a single-sex context?

3. Have you had any experiences in which a person's personal story has given you a new understanding of their religious perspective?

4. How might you arrange the use of personal story in the context of a dialogue event?

5. Is dialogue a distraction from effective social action, or a precondition for it?

6. Does your own experience support O'Neill's view that intrafaith relationships are often harder to manage than interfaith ones? What challenges would you anticipate if you wanted to facilitate a dialogue between people on different parts of the spectrum of one religion? What could you do to manage those challenges?

7. What steps might be taken to involve more conservative religious people in interreligious dialogue?

Bibliography

Birmingham Mail. 'Your Community: Sharing love between our city's faiths.' Accessed 21st May, 2012. http://www.birminghammail.net/news/your-news/2010/11/02/your-community-sharing-love-between-our-city-s-faiths-97319-27585594/.

Churches Together. Accessed 22nd May, 2012. http://www.churches-together.net/Groups/42314/Churches_Together_in.aspx.

Darling, Justine. *Restorative Justice: A Tool in Rebuilding Post-Conflict Northern Ireland.* DigitalCollections@SIT, 2012. Accessed 22nd May, 2013. http://digitalcollections.sit.edu/conflict_reconcilation_symposium/jan11/memoryhealingpanel/3/.

Dialogue Society. *Making Dialogue Effective.* London: Dialogue Society, 2013. Available on the Dialogue Society website, http://www.dialoguesociety.org/publications/Making-Dialogue-Effective.pdf.

Feast, The. Accessed 22nd May, 2012. http://www.thefeast.org.uk/about/history/.

Lohre, Kathryn. 'Women's Interfaith Initiatives in the United States Post 9/11.' *Interreligious Insight* 5, no. 2 (2007).

O'Neill, Maura. *Mending a Torn World: Women in Interreligious Dialogue (Faith Meets Faith).* New York: Orbis Books, 2007.

O'Neill, Maura. *Women Speaking, Women Listening: Women in Interreligious Dialogue.* New York: Orbis Books, 1990.

Public Conversation Project. 'Fostering Dialogue Across Divides.' Accessed 22nd May, 2012. http://www.publicconversations.org/docs/resources/Jams_website.pdf.

St Ethelburga's Centre for Reconciliation and Peace. 'Evangelicals explore interfaith encounter at St Ethelburga's.' Accessed 22nd May, 2012. http://stethelburgas.org/evangelicals-explore-interfaith-encounter-st-ethelburgas.

St Ethelburga's Centre for Reconciliation and Peace. 'What's your story?' Accessed 22nd May, 2012. http://stethelburgas.org/narrative-resource.

Tetlow, Ruth. 'The Missing Dimension: Women and Inter Faith Encounter in Birmingham.' *Current Dialogue* 46 (2005).

Recommended Reading

O'Neill's Works:

O'Neill, Maura. *Mending a Torn World: Women in Interreligious Dialogue (Faith Meets Faith)*. New York: Orbis Books, 2007.

O'Neill, Maura. *Women Speaking, Women Listening: Women in Interreligious Dialogue*. New York: Orbis Books, 1990.

Practical Applications:

Golan, Galia, and Zahira Kamal. 'Women's People-to-People Activities: Do We Do It Better?' *Palestine-Israel Journal of Politics, Economics and Culture* 12/13:4/1 (2005). http://www.pij.org/details.php?id=403.

Lohre, Kathryn. 'Women's Interfaith Initiatives in the United States Post 9/11.' *Interreligious Insight* 5:2 (2007).

McCreary, Alf. *In War and Peace: The Story of Corrymeela*. Belfast: Brehon Press Ltd, 2007.

Mollenkott, Virginia Ramey ed. *Women of Faith in Dialogue*. New York: Crossroad, 1987.

Montague, Mary. *Relationships to Reconciliation*. The Corrymeela Community: 2000.

Public Conversations Project. 'Fostering Dialogue Across Divides.' Accessed 22nd May, 2012. http://www.publicconversations.org/docs/resources/Jams_website.pdf.

Tetlow, Ruth. 'The Missing Dimension: Women and Inter Faith Encounter in Birmingham.' *Current Dialogue* 46 (2005).

Daniel Yankelovich

Biographical Introduction

Daniel Yankelovich is a renowned American public opinion analyst and social scientist. He was born in Boston, Massachusetts in 1924. He studied at Harvard where he gained his bachelor's and master's degrees. After pursuing further studies at the Sorbonne in Paris he stayed in academia and taught as a Professor of Psychology first at New York University and then at the New School for Social Research, New York. He holds honorary doctorates from Washington University and George Washington University. He left academia for a time in 1958 to found his own marketing and research firm. In 1975 he co-founded the not-for-profit organisation Public Agenda, which promotes public engagement in democracy, group reflection and problem solving. He also founded the New York Times/ Yankelovich Poll which later became the New York Times/CBS poll. He is the founder and chairman of the business research firm DYG Inc and of Viewpoint Learning, which facilitates dialogue for business and public policy clients. During his career he has held directorships at a range of prestigious firms and he is the author of nine books as well as numerous articles.[1]

In his influential book *The Magic of Dialogue*, Yankelovich notes that, as with so many of the significant thinkers on dialogue who have emerged from a wide range of professions, his discovery of the transformative power of dialogue grew directly out of work in his own field.[2] Public opinion research showed him that, contrary to the conventional view, public opinion does not simply develop through the analysis of facts supplied by the media, but through a process of dialogue. Again contrary to the conventional view, he found that the interplay of facts, values and feelings in this process often leads to considerable wisdom in public judgement. His experience on the boards of various organisations similarly showed that 'in the crunch, on the issues that really count, where the future of the institution is at stake... it is dialogue rather than factual analysis that most engages board members and shapes their judgement.'[3] His experience in both contexts underlined a crucial insight: the better our dialogue skills the wiser the judgements we reach through dialogue. In his writings and practical endeavours he has sought to elucidate and build capacity for skilful dialogue.

---

1   'Daniel Yankelovich Papers,' Thomas J. Dodd Research Center, University of Connecticut, accessed 1ˢᵗ August, 2012, http://doddcenter.uconn.edu/asc/findaids/Yankelovich/ MSS19950027.html#d0e38.

2   Daniel Yankelovich, *The Magic of Dialogue* (New York: Simon and Schuster, 1999), 23ff.

3   Yankelovich, *The Magic of Dialogue*, 27.

Yankelovich's thought on dialogue is intimately connected to his vision of a reinvigorated American democracy and his efforts to build this. While his understanding of dialogue per se is examined in most depth in *The Magic of Dialogue*, *Coming to Public Judgement*, published eight years before, already suggested dialogical solutions to the crisis faced by American democracy.[4] Experts dominated political decision processes, while the public felt that they could have no real impact on policy and often disengaged from politics in consequence. To address this imbalance, Yankelovich suggested that the public's role should be strengthened by developing techniques and structures to help the public come to reflected, stable judgement, as opposed to ill-considered opinion. The techniques he proposed were dialogical processes in which ordinary people could 'work through' difficult social and political issues. He continued to explore these processes in practice with colleagues at Public Agenda, Viewpoint Learning and partner organisations. *Towards Wiser Public Judgement*, published in 2012, edited by Yankelovich and his colleague Will Friedman, reviews methods developed through this practice.

---

4   Daniel Yankelovich, *Coming to Public Judgement* (Syracuse, New York: Syracuse University Press), 1991.

Thought on Dialogue

As suggested by the title of his book, *The Magic of Dialogue*, Yankelovich considers dialogue to have unique and highly valuable properties. It can 'strengthen(s) relationships and trust, forge(s) alliances, find(s) truths that bind us together, and bring(s) people into alignment on goals and strategies.'[5] He affirms Buber's insight that in dialogue we reach beyond the confines of self to an authentic encounter with the other.[6] Dialogue is a way of being and a way of building relationship. He emphasises, though, that 'dialogue is not... an arcane and esoteric form of intellectual exercise that only the few can play. It is a practical, everyday tool accessible to us all.'[7] Dialogue is a particular kind of talk which requires particular competencies and strategies, some of which are explored in Yankelovich's book.

This section will focus largely on Yankelovich's examination of dialogue in *The Magic of Dialogue,* since it is here that he gives his most considered and comprehensive exploration of dialogue per se. We will explore Yankelovich's definition of dialogue, which he considers reflects what most serious practitioners mean when they use the word. We will take a look at some of the practical strategies for dialogue that he proposes and some of the barriers to dialogue that he outlines. First, though, it is worth noting the crucial role that Yankelovich sees for dialogue in contemporary society.

Yankelovich sees dialogue as a key part of the remedy to a number of interconnected social problems in his own American society. He sees America as suffering from a disturbing tendency towards a 'culture of technical control', 'a mindset... that treats people as objects to be manipulated.'[8] Under the pressures of modern lifestyles, people become trapped in separate compartments, 'silos', according to status, politics, ethnicity, beliefs, language and so on. In addition to being isolated, ordinary people are left disempowered and politically unengaged by the sense of the almost complete separation of experts and elites from the general public.

Dialogue has a unique ability to forge channels of communication and understanding between people separated by difference and depersonalisation, responding to a fundamental need in modern society.[9] Further, it can help to

---

5   Yankelovich, *The Magic of Dialogue,* 217.

6   Yankelovich, *Coming to Public Judgement,* 239 f, *The Magic of Dialogue,* 14 f.

7   Yankelovich, *The Magic of Dialogue,* 15.

8   Yankelovich, *The Magic of Dialogue,* 157.

9   Part III of *The Magic of Dialogue* (149ff) explores how dialogue might play a key role in revitalising American democracy and addressing the various 'cultural faultlines' of contemporary society.

reinvigorate democracy, redressing the balance between elites and the public by strengthening the position of the latter. Public opinion should play an important role in informing policy in a healthy democracy.[10] However, shallow and unstable public opinion cannot perform that role. What is needed is public judgement, in which the public 'accepts responsibility for the consequences of its views' and holds them consistently over time.[11] The public does not arrive at such judgement automatically when bombarded with a great deal of information. It needs to 'work through' issues dialogically.[12] Facilitated dialogue processes can accelerate the process by which the public work through issues and come to judgment. Such processes are particularly needed to help the American public get to grips with a host of highly urgent contemporary issues, notably the challenge of providing energy sustainably without irreparable environmental damage, and managing 'troubled relations with the Muslim world.'[13]

We now turn to Yankelovich's definition of dialogue. He clarifies the differences between dialogue, debate, discussion and deliberation. The difference between dialogue and debate is clear. In debate you aim to win an argument. Dialogue is about mutual understanding, and 'the worst possible way to advance mutual understanding is to win debating points at the expense of others.'[14]

The relationship between dialogue and discussion is more subtle. Talk becomes dialogue rather than just discussion when three particular conditions are in place.[15] Firstly, there must be equality between the participants, and an absence of coercive influences. Even if outside the dialogue they have very different social or professional status, for dialogue to work they have to try to put this aside so that

---

10   Yankelovich shares this position with Jürgen Habermas; see our chapter on Habermas in this volume.

11   Yankelovich, *Coming to Public Judgment,* 24.

12   Yankelovich, *Coming to Public Judgment,* 59 ff; Daniel Yankelovich and Will Friedman eds., *Towards Wiser Public Judgement,* (Nashville, Texas: Vanderbilt University Press, 2010), 18 f.

13   Yankelovich and Friedman eds., *Toward Wiser Public Judgment,* 20 ff, 29 ff.

14   Yankelovich, *The Magic of Dialogue,* 38.

15   Yankelovich, *The Magic of Dialogue,* 41 ff.

all can participate freely, without fear of any form of intimidation.[16] Secondly, dialogue requires us to listen with empathy. For dialogue to happen we need the ability 'to think someone else's thoughts and feel someone else's feelings.'[17] This demands considerable motivation and patience.

Finally, in dialogue participants need to explore their own assumptions and those of others, and bring them out into the open. Our deeply engrained assumptions about the world and other people can very effectively prevent us from understanding other points of view. As David Bohm notes, we tend to identify our assumptions very strongly with ourselves, and feel attacked when they are commented on or challenged by others.[18] However, in a real dialogue participants suspend judgement when assumptions come to light, allowing these assumptions to be explored in safety. To recap, discussion does not necessarily require equality, listening with empathy or the exploration of assumptions, but these three conditions are the marks of dialogue.

Deliberation, Yankelovich considers, is 'a form of thought and reflection that can take place in any kind of conversation.' It is a problem solving activity involving the weighing up of different options.[19] This activity can happen, according to Yankelovich, in dialogue as well as in discussion or debate. It is only when imminent consensus and decision become the priority of the conversation that dialogue's

---

16   Yankelovich's vision of dialogue reflects Habermas's notion of communicative action in which people speak together in order to achieve understanding and move toward collaboration, and emphatically not to coerce or manipulate one another. Yankelovich's thought is influenced by that of Habermas, which he discusses in *Coming to Public Judgment,* see especially 215 ff. Like Habermas, Yankelovich appears to have very high expectations for dialogue. It seems well nigh impossible for power imbalances to be entirely cast aside. Nevertheless, facilitators can at least attempt to move the situation in the direction of equality, for instance through thoughtful recruitment, ground rules, the example they set and interventions during the process. Alison Kadlec and Will Friedman explore practical strategies for ensuring inclusive and egalitarian processes in their article 'Deliberative Democracy and the Problem of Power,' *Journal of Public Deliberation* 3, no. 1(2007).

17   Yankelovich, *The Magic of Dialogue,* 43.

18   Yankelovich, *The Magic of Dialogue,* 45.

19   Yankelovich, *The Magic of Dialogue,* 37. Definitions of deliberation, as distinguished from dialogue, are given by the National Coalition for Dialogue and Deliberation: http://ncdd. org/rc/what-are-dd (accessed 2nd August, 2012), and by Ute Kelly and Lisa Cumming in *Civil Society Supporting Dialogue and Deliberation,* (Carnegie UK Trust, 2010), 7. These definitions differ from Yankelovich's approach in that they present dialogue and deliberation as separate, though related, kinds of conversation. Kelly and Cumming cite Levine's specification that deliberation at least in aspiration, "aims toward a reasoned consensus."' Yankelovich does not seem to see consensus as an essential aim of deliberation.

essential focus on mutual understanding gets lost. Dialogue, though it often leads to decision-making processes, must be kept separate from these for each to function properly.[20]

Yankelovich's very practically-oriented book examines a range of examples from his own experience, mostly drawn from the world of management, and draws out key lessons and practical strategies for promoting quality dialogue. We will include below Yankelovich's summary of the fifteen strategies he identifies, but first let us briefly explore some of these in the contexts of the case studies from which he abstracts them.

One of the cases discussed is a conversation at a meeting of the trustees of a prestigious research institute. In the course of the conversation tension arose between the business trustees, who felt that the institute was becoming too specialised, and the academic trustees, who were all specialists and believed that specialisation was essential for the institute's success. A breakthrough came with a comment from one of the business trustees. He noted that the other business trustees were all generalists who were naturally uncomfortable with specialisation, but that specialisation had actually made the institute great. He ended by saying, 'So if we are uncomfortable, that's probably a sign that the institute is doing something right.' Essentially, he recognised the limitations of the perspective of his own group. He thereby cleared the way for a real dialogue. Everybody laughed, the tension was broken, and people were able to start empathising with each other and exploring their common challenges.[21]

Let us turn to the strategies that Yankelovich draws out of this example. One of them is this: 'Clarify assumptions that lead to subculture distortions.'[22] People have different sets of values and preoccupations depending on their different subcultures – the particular professional, social and cultural groups to which they belong. These assumptions can create all kinds of tensions. We need to identify them in order for dialogue to work. This is exactly what the business trustee in the example managed to do.

Note too how helpful it was that the business trustee focused on the assumptions of his own group. In recognising our own assumptions we make ourselves a little vulnerable and people often respond by becoming more empathetic and open. Identifying other people's assumptions can easily offend them. Yankelovich suggests another strategy: 'Bring forth your own assumptions before speculating on those of others.'[23]

---

20   Yankelovich, *The Magic of Dialogue*, 56f.

21   Yankelovich, *The Magic of Dialogue*, 59ff.

22   Yankelovich, *The Magic of Dialogue*, 65.

23   Yankelovich, *The Magic of Dialogue*, 66f.

In a rather different example he discusses a public conversation on parental involvement in education, run by Public Agenda. A man turned up who had not been invited and was known as a difficult character. At the start of the meeting he directed a couple of unfriendly comments towards some of the teachers present, but later he seemed to settle into the spirit of the dialogue, waiting his turn and listening to others. Having been allowed to participate, he started to appreciate the fairness with which the meeting was run. At the end he shook hands with the head teacher and thanked her. The dialogue was constructive and a relationship was mended.

Yankelovich suggests this strategy: 'Err on the side of including people who disagree.'[24] If we only include those who agree with us, the dialogue might boost everyone's morale, but it will not help heal any divisions. Including those who disagree makes a dialogue more authentic and credible and gives it a chance to effect reconciliation.

The full list of practical dialogue strategies identified by Yankelovich is as follows:[25]

1. Err of the side of including people who disagree. *Taking a risk often pays off, bringing greater mutual understanding between divided groups and individuals.*

2. Initiate dialogue through a gesture of empathy. *Acknowledging 'the legitimacy of the point of view of the other' often breaks down barriers of defensiveness and allows dialogue to begin.*[26]

3. Check for the presence of all three core requirements of dialogue – equality, empathic listening, and surfacing assumptions nonjudgmentally – and learn how to introduce the missing ones. *Without the presence of all three there can be no real dialogue.*

4. Minimize the level of mistrust before pursuing practical objectives. *Efforts towards cooperation will be futile without a certain level of trust.*

5. Keep dialogue and decision making compartmentalized. *They are different kinds of process and if confused will undermine each other.*[27]

6. Focus on common interests, not divisive ones. *Concentrating on shared interests is more conducive to dialogue.*

---

24   Yankelovich, *The Magic of Dialogue,* 103f, 107f.

25   Yankelovich, *The Magic of Dialogue,* 127f. The strategies are given in Yankelovich's words. Brief further explanation by the current authors is given in italics.

26   Yankelovich, *The Magic of Dialogue,* 105.

27   Yankelovich, *The Magic of Dialogue,* 57.

7. Use specific cases to raise general issues. *Referring to concrete examples helps people to appreciate the issues at stake.*

8. Bring forth your own assumptions before speculating on those of others. *Highlighting the assumptions of others can easily sound accusatory, whereas recognising one's own sets a helpful example of self-awareness and openness.*

9. Clarify assumptions that lead to subculture distortions. *When the assumptions associated with particular subcultures are shaping a conversation without this being recognised, tactfully identifying them can bring helpful clarity.*

10. Where applicable, identify mistrust as the real source of misunderstandings. *Mistrust prevents openness and inhibits dialogue. Sometimes simply recognising that this is happening is enough to help people overcome it and converse more openly.*

11. Expose old scripts to a reality check. *We interpret reality through 'the web of beliefs, values, assumption and customs that have shaped our views over decades of experience.*[28] *It is valuable to bring assumptions to the surface; sometimes when we do, we see that they are no longer valid and need to be amended.*

12. Focus on conflicts between value systems, not people. *Avoid stereotyping people according to their subculture.*

13. Be sure trust exists before addressing transference distortions. *Sometimes the dynamics of previous relationships interfere with current ones. For example, the experience of being taken advantage of by a relative may make a person touchy when a colleague asks her to do something outside her official role. Bringing such 'transference distortions' into the open can explain and ease mysterious tensions between people. However, examining these 'ghosts' of past relationships can be personally threatening, and it should not be attempted where there is not a relationship of trust.*[29]

14. When appropriate, express the emotions that accompany strongly held values. *Emotions are a legitimate and important part of the process of dialogue.*

---

28   Yankelovich, *The Magic of Dialogue,* 108 f.

29   Yankelovich, *The Magic of Dialogue,* 87.

15. Encourage relationships in order to humanise transactions. *Encountering one another as individuals on a human level breaks down stereotypes and hostility.*[30]

As well as identifying positive strategies for dialogue in his book, Yankelovich explores some 'potholes of the mind'. Most dialogue participants, he suggests, will find it easier to adopt the strategies than to get over their own 'potholes', 'deeply engrained habits that undermine dialogue'.[31] He lists ten. We can briefly summarise them here. One problem is holding back, being unwilling to take the risk of speaking. Another is 'being locked in a box', being unable to see beyond the restrictions of the same old ideas and solutions. People might tend to move towards action prematurely, cutting the dialogue short, or they might be inclined to listen without hearing, being 'unwilling to make an extra effort to understand others when they are not wholly articulate.' It can be difficult when people start at different points, with some having explored an issue deeply while others have barely started to grasp it. Another problem occurs when people cannot resist 'showboating', showing off their knowledge, toughness or intelligence at the expense of real dialogue. Some people find it difficult to break the habit, engrained in the practice of many professions, of scoring debating points at others' expense. Others cannot resist the game of constantly adopting a contrary point of view. Some people are unable to go beyond discussion of their own pet preoccupation. Similarly, some leaders find it difficult to really listen to other dialogue participants because they are so concerned with pushing their constituents' interests.

Yankelovich suggests a number of steps that participants and facilitators can take to counter these problems. Sometimes a facilitator can make progress just by recognising the potholes that come with certain participants and making small adjustments, such as providing icebreakers to help those who tend to hold back, or giving a little extra time so that somebody can do their 'showboating' and then settle down to real dialogue. Individuals will sometimes overcome their particular

---

30   Yankelovich's dialogue strategies are more numerous and subtle than the list of guidelines one might introduce to participants at the beginning of a dialogue session. A workable set of 'Guide lines for Dialogue' is given on the website of Viewpoint Learning. They are as follows: 1. The purpose of dialogue is to understand and learn from one another. You cannot "win" a dialogue. 2. All dialogue participants speak for themselves, not as representatives of groups or special interests. 3. Treat everyone in a dialogue as an equal: leave role, status and stereotypes at the door. 4. Be open and listen to others even when you disagree; try not to rush to judgment. 5. Search for assumptions (especially your own). 6. Look for common ground. 7. Keep dialogue and decision-making separate (dialogue comes first). Viewpoint Learning, accessed 19th April, 2012, http://www.viewpointlearning.com/about-us/ground-rules-for-dialogue/.

31   Yankelovich, *The Magic of Dialogue,* 129 ff.

potholes in the course of the dialogue, where there is time for this. Some may also benefit from individual training where they have the necessary motivation.[32]

In *The Magic of Dialogue* Yankelovich anticipates a growing readiness to devote time and energy to dialogue and the development of the skills needed for it because it addresses pressing needs in contemporary society. This prediction is to some extent borne out by the growth of a new social movement which he comments on a decade later in *Toward Wiser Public Judgment*. This movement seeks to reinvigorate democracy through a range of more or less dialogical initiatives.[33] In the next section we will take a look at the efforts of Yankelovich, his colleagues and others to harness the 'magic' of dialogue for the good of society and the health of democracy.[34]

---

32 Yankelovich notes a number of American organisations providing such training. See *The Magic of Dialogue*, 143.

33 Yankelovich and Friedman eds., *Toward Wiser Public Judgment*, 25 f.

34 Yankelovich, *The Magic of Dialogue*, 217.

Theory and Practice

Yankelovich's theory of dialogue comes from concrete experience, some of which was gained through the work of the non-profit organisation Public Agenda, which he co-founded in 1975. His insights continue to feed back into the practice of Public Agenda and of his company Viewpoint Learning, founded in 1999, which facilitates various forms of dialogue for business and public policy clients.[35] In the work of these organisations, Yankelovich's vision of how dialogue can help revitalise democracy is put to the test.

This section will focus on the work of Public Agenda and its partners. We will explore their methods and look at a case study. We will also touch on some of the possibilities and challenges for the further development of this kind of work, and note the development of a new 'deliberative democracy movement' composed of similar initiatives.

Public Agenda's first involvement in community dialogue was in its support of the National Issues Forums (NIFs), a nationwide network of forums facilitating public conversations on important issues ranging from civil rights to health care reform. Yankelovich, along with David Mathews of the Kettering Foundation[36], was instrumental in the development of these forums and Public Agenda provided issue guides to inform the conversations. Public Agenda has since developed its own public engagement processes, along with resources and training to support them, but these processes and the NIFs both use a kind of dialogue called 'choicework'.

In choicework, participants are divided into small, diverse groups of ten to fifteen people, with specially trained local facilitators. They are presented with several different approaches to a particular issue or problem. Issue guides or a presentation provide sufficient information for participants to grasp the issue. These resources are presented in language that will make sense to participants and in terms relevant to their experience. Participants consider which approach they favour and explain their reasons to each other. In the course of this exchange, people gradually adjust their perspectives to absorb the complexity of the issue which is revealed by people's diverse viewpoints and experiences. Ultimately the group considers possible ideas

---

35   Notably, Viewpoint Learning provides stakeholders with a better understanding of public opinion through day-long dialogues in which groups of citizens 'work through' issues: http://www.viewpointlearning.com, accessed 2nd August, 2012; Steven A. Rosell and Heidi Gantwerk, 'Moving Beyond Polls and Focus Groups,' in *Towards Wiser Public Judgement,* ed. Yankelovich and Friedman, 110 ff.

36   http://www.kettering.org, accessed 19th April, 2012. The Kettering Foundation is 'a research institution devoted to trying to find ways to increase citizen participation in society, by asking the question; "What does it take to make democracy work as it should?"'

for action and potential next steps. Finally the groups come together to share key elements of their conversations.[37]

For community dialogues to work effectively, painstaking planning is required. Public Agenda conducts considerable preliminary research to make sure that issues are framed in a helpful and engaging way. To be authentic, and trusted by diverse participants, the process must be 'owned' by a local planning team, comprising representatives of groups with differing perspectives. Careful recruitment of participants and the selection and training of suitable local facilitators are crucial in order to include all sectors of the community and to achieve an environment of equality in which all participants genuinely have a voice.[38]

Real progress in mutual understanding has been consistently observed in both Public Agenda dialogues and in the NIFs. Reflecting on the NIFs, practitioners involved note that while opinions may not be changed, choicework participants develop a more mature understanding of the 'costs and consequences of different courses of action', and 'of why others' opinions differed from their own.'[39] A comment from a participant in a Public Agenda community dialogue on education reflects how satisfying this process can be: 'Having a conversation like this totally takes you outside the box… you're able to hear other people's ideas about what's going on, and also you're able to share your ideas, so I think that this was magnificent.'[40] Participants make progress in 'working through' an issue and consequently leave as more 'aware and confident citizens' who are better able 'to inform and support relevant public policies.'[41] Further, while dialogues like these might not give policy makers a clear indication of majority opinion on a specific issue, they tend to highlight the values, concerns and priorities that citizens share, and which should be reflected in the policies of truly democratic leaders.[42]

In addition to these immediate benefits, public dialogues may inspire action by different individuals and organisations, build connections between diverse groups and have a lasting impact on local political culture. In Bridgeport, Connecticut, a

---

37   Daniel Yankelovich and Will Friedman eds., *Towards Wiser Public Judgement,* 56ff, 83.

38   Alison Kadlec and Will Friedman, 'Thirty-Five Years of Working on Public Judgement at Public Agenda,' in *Towards Wiser Public Judgement,* ed. Yankelovich and Friedman, 79ff.

39   Keith Melville and Robert J Kingston, 'The Experience of the National Issues Forums,' in *Towards Wiser Public Judgement,* ed. Yankelovich and Friedman, 63.

40   'Achieving the Dream Communications: Communications Part 2' video, Public Agenda, accessed 27th April, 2012, http://www.publicagenda.org/media/multimedia.

41   Will Friedman, 'Coming to Public Judgment,' in *Towards Wiser Public Judgment,* ed. Yankelovich and Friedman, 138.

42   Melville and Kingston, in 'The Experience of the National Issues Forums,' 71.

community choicework dialogue on education supported by Public Agenda sparked a series of dozens of similar dialogues on different topics arranged by enthusiastic local organisers; the local community developed a lasting capacity for community dialogue. Local policy makers gradually became more inclined to engage with citizens' perspectives and the community developed an ethos of responsibility and 'an ability to hold leaders accountable in reasonable ways.'[43] The dialogues on education led to hundreds of new volunteers in schools, renewed efforts by schools to engage with parents and beneficial new policies. Clear improvements in educational attainment were seen in the town, perhaps due not only to concrete changes in schools but also to the beneficial effects of a surrounding culture of active engagement with civic and community life.[44] The Bridgeport dialogues powerfully demonstrate the potential of community dialogue initiatives to bring about real social change.

Will Friedman, the President of Public Agenda, sees two main challenges ahead for this and similar organisations in their efforts to enhance the quality of democracy: 'ensuring that efforts to support public judgment lead to significant impacts; and scaling up deliberative work from the local level, where it has been applied most successfully, to the level of national politics.'[45] Regarding the first challenge, Friedman explains that while it would be foolish to obligate policy makers to implement every recommendation coming from public deliberation, they do need to be accountable to the participants in some way if the latter are going to trust that their participation counts. Policy makers should be expected to continue a dialogue with citizens and 'say why they choose to respond more to some [ideas] and less to others.'[46] Concerning the challenge of bringing dialogical and deliberative processes to the level of national politics, Friedman highlights three avenues to explore: the potential for the media, notably 'new media', to serve a role in helping

---

43   Kadlec and Friedman, 'Thirty-Five Years of Working on Public Judgement at Public Agenda,' 90.

44   Kadlec and Friedman, 'Thirty-Five Years of Working on Public Judgement at Public Agenda,' 93.

45   Friedman, 'Coming to Public Judgment,' 131.

46   Friedman 'Coming to Public Judgment,' 136.

      The Sustainable Communities Act is an interesting UK example of a mechanism requiring government to listen to and negotiate on proposals from citizens, while not being obliged to implement them. Local Works, accessed 2nd February, 2013, http://www.localworks. org/pages/the-sustainable-communities-act.

      Friedman refers readers to examples of 'deliberative processes tied to concrete outcomes via the post-deliberation exercise of various forms of power' in Archon Fung, *Empowered Deliberation: Reinventing Urban Democracy* (Princeton, NJ: Princeton University Press, 2006).

the public work through issues and develop public judgment; the potential for 'the institutions that touch us all', namely schools and workplaces, to introduce practices that will develop skills in dialogue and deliberation; and the potential of local public engagement initiatives gradually to build capacity and demand for 'a truly national deliberative politics.'[47]

The organisations founded by Yankelovich do not stand alone in their efforts to reinvigorate democracy through dialogical processes. Efforts on this front have attained the proportions of something of a movement.[48] National networks such as the Deliberative Democracy Consortium and the National Coalition for Dialogue and Deliberation facilitate the sharing of ideas and resources across organisations.[49] Everyday Democracy and Search for Common Ground are two examples taken from a large pool of organisations.[50]

The 'deliberative democracy movement' is primarily a North American and Canadian phenomenon. However, there are dialogue initiatives using similar methods in the United Kingdom, although they are less prominent and less connected. The Transition movement uses dialogue and deliberation to seek community led responses to the challenges of climate change and peak oil.[51] Bradford University's Programme for a Peaceful City has used various forms of public conversation to build understanding between diverse participants on divisive issues.[52] 'Reading the Riots', the major research project run by the Guardian newspaper and the London School of Economics following the civil disorder of

---

47   Friedman in *Towards Wiser Public Judgement*, ed. Yankelovich and Friedman, 139 ff; 145.

48   See Yankelovich and Friedman eds., *Toward Wiser Public Judgment*, 25 f. It is worth noting that while Yankelovich considers this movement an exciting and very important development, he 'winces' at the name given to it by leading participants: 'the deliberative democracy movement'. The term 'deliberative' suggests a process that is essentially rational, whereas in his experience dialogical processes essentially involve emotions and irrational elements. (He adopts a rather more holistic approach than Habermas.)

      On the deliberative democracy movement see also: Ute Kelly and Lisa Cumming, *Civil Society Supporting Dialogue and Deliberation*, (Carnegie UK Trust, 2010), 31; Martha L. McCoy and Patrick L Scully, 'Deliberative Dialogue to Expand Civil Engagement: What Kind of Talk Does Democracy Need?' *National Civic Review* 91 (Summer 2002): 117.

49   Deliberative Democracy Consortium, accessed 5th March, 2013, http://www.deliberative-democracy.net/; National Consortium for Dialogue and Deliberation, accessed 5th March, 2013, Ncdd.org.

50   Everyday Democracy, accessed 5th March, 2013, http://www.everyday-democracy.org (Everyday Democracy was formerly called the Study Circles Resource Centre); Search for Common Ground, accessed 5th March, 2013, http://www.sfcg.org.

51   Kelly and Cumming, *Civil Society Supporting Dialogue and Deliberation*, 16.

52   Kelly and Cumming, *Civil Society Supporting Dialogue and Deliberation*, 11.

August 2011, included a number of 'community conversations' in riot-affected cities.[53] The Dialogue Society's 'Community Engagement Dinners' manual gives practical advice on getting community dialogue started through local dinner and discussion evenings.[54] Ute Kelly and Lisa Cumming, in their report for the Carnegie Trust, explore how civil society might support the growth of dialogue and deliberation in the UK and how these processes, facilitated on a large scale, could help to address some of the major challenges facing our society.[55] Yankelovich is by no means alone in appealing to the 'magic' of dialogue to address democratic deficiencies, social ills and intractable political and environmental dilemmas.

---

53   'Reading the Riots launches Community Conversations,' the Guardian, 8th February, 2012, accessed 18th March, 2013, http://www.guardian.co.uk/uk/2012/feb/08/reading-the-riots-community-conversations.

54   The manual can be downloaded from the Dialogue Society website, http://www.dialoguesociety.org/publications/community/653-community-engagement-dinners.html.

55   Kelly and Cumming, Civil Society Supporting Dialogue and Deliberation, 29ff.

Questions for Reflection

1. Have you ever been struck by the 'magic' of dialogue? In what context? Was it the kind of dialogue that Yankelovich (or one of the other thinkers in this volume) describes?

2. Does your experience support Yankelovich's argument that it is through a process of dialogue with others that we come to judgement about political issues?

3. If you were facilitating a dialogue, what steps might you take to ensure the presence of each of Yankelovich's three key conditions (equality; listening with empathy; surfacing assumptions)?

4. What might you do to avoid or respond to the following potholes? [56]

    a. Some participants holding back, being unwilling to take the risk of saying anything.

    b. People 'starting at different points'.

    c. People listening without hearing, being 'unwilling to make an extra effort to understand others when they are not wholly articulate.'

    d. People 'showboating' - showing off knowledge, toughness or intelligence at the expense of real dialogue.

5. Would the 'choicework' dialogue techniques used by Yankelovich and his colleagues work as well in countries other than the United States?

6. What proportion of the population would dialogue initiatives have to reach to have a real impact on the health of a democracy? What would it take for such efforts to reach that proportion of the population (in terms of civil society effort, political will, time, resources etc)?

---

56   Yankelovich, *The Magic of Dialogue*, 129 ff.

Bibliography

Deliberative Democracy Consortium, The. Accessed 5th March, 2013. http://www.deliberative-democracy.net/.

Dialogue Society. 'Community Engagement Dinners.' Accessed 1st August, 2012. http://www.dialoguesociety.org/publications/community/653-community-engagement-dinners.html.

Dialogos. Accessed 27th April, 2012. http://www.dialogos.com.

Everyday Democracy. Accessed 5th March, 2013. http://www.everyday-democracy.org.

Fung, Archon. *Empowered Deliberation: Reinventing Urban Democracy.* Princeton, NJ: Princeton University Press.

Kadlec, Alison and Will Friedman. 'Deliberative Democracy and the Problem of Power.' *Journal of Public Deliberation* 3, no. 1 (2007).

Kelly, Ute and Lisa Cumming. *Civil Society Supporting Dialogue and Deliberation.* Carnegie UK Trust, 2010.

Kettering Foundation. Accessed 19th April, 2012. http://kettering.org/.

McCoy, Martha L., and Patrick L Scully. 'Deliberative Dialogue to Expand Civil Engagement: What Kind of Talk Does Democracy Need?' *National Civic Review* 91 (Summer 2002): 117-135.

National Coalition for Dialogue and Deliberation. Accessed 5th March, 2013. Ncdd.org.

Public Agenda. Accessed 27th April, 2012. http://www.publicagenda.org/.

Public Agenda. 'Achieving the Dream: Communications Part 2' video. Accessed 27th April, 2012. http://www.publicagenda.org/media/multimedia.

Search for Common Ground. Accessed 5th March, 2013. http://www.sfcg.org

Thomas J. Dodd Research Center, University of Connecticut. 'Daniel Yankelovich Papers.' Accessed 1st August, 2012. http://doddcenter.uconn.edu/asc/findaids/Yankelovich/MSS19950027.html#d0e38.

Viewpoint Learning. Accessed 19th April, 2012. http://www.viewpointlearning.com/.

Yankelovich, Daniel. *Coming to Public Judgement.* Syracuse, New York: Syracuse University Press, 1991.

Yankelovich, Daniel. *The Magic of Dialogue.* New York: Simon and Schuster, 1999.

Yankelovich, Daniel, and Will Friedman eds. *Towards Wiser Public Judgement.* Nashville, Texas: Vanderbilt University Press, 2010.

Recommended Reading

Yankelovich's Works:

Yankelovich, Daniel. *Coming to Public Judgement.* Syracuse: Syracuse University Press, 1991.

Yankelovich, Daniel. *The Magic of Dialogue.* New York: Simon and Schuster, 1999.

Yankelovich, Daniel. 'The Magic of Dialogue.' National Head Start Bulletin 68 (2000):13-14. Reproduced on Athealth.com, accessed 19th April, 2012, http://www.athealth.com/Consumer/disorders/dialogue.html.

Yankelovich, Daniel and Will Friedman eds. *Toward Wiser Public Judgement.* Nashville, Texas: Vanderbilt University Press, 2011.

Practical Applications:

Carter Center. 'Democratic Dialogue – Annotated Bibliography.' 2003. Available on the Democratic Dialogue Network website, accessed 20th April, 2012, http://www.democraticdialoguenetwork.org/documents.pl?s=1&ss=11&page=2.

Heierbacher, Sandy. 'Dialogue and Deliberation Methods.' National Coalition for Dialogue and Deliberation, 12th September, 2010. Accessed 18th March, 2013. http://ncdd.org/rc/item/4856.

Kadlec, Alison and Will Friedman. 'Deliberative Democracy and the Problem of Power.' *Journal of Public Deliberation* 3, no. 1 (2007).

Kelly, Ute and Lisa Cumming. *Civil Society Supporting Dialogue and Deliberation.* Carnegie UK Trust, 2010. Available online at http://www.brad.ac.uk/ssis/media/SSIS/Documents/Civil_society_supporting_dialogue_and_Deliberation.pdf.

McCoy, Martha L. and Patrick L Scully. 'Deliberative Dialogue to Expand Civil Engagement: What Kind of Talk Does Democracy Need?' *National Civic Review* 91 (Summer 2002): 117-135.

Public Agenda. Accessed 27th April, 2012. http://www.publicagenda.org/.

Viewpoint Learning. Accessed 19th April, 2012. http://www.viewpointlearning.com/.